Accelerated Learning Techniques for Students

Learn More in Less Time!

DR. JOE MCCULLOUGH

Dedication

This book is dedicated to my two-year-old daughter, Aria. May you never lose your love of learning or your passion for exploring life's many wonders.

Table of Contents

Dedication..iii

Table of Contents...iv

Acknowledgements...8

Introduction..9

Part 1: The Five Steps of Accelerated Learning

Meet Your Amazing Brain 16
   The Triune Brain...17
   The Brain Stem or Reptilian Brain.............................18
   The Limbic System or Mammalian Brain...................20
   The Neocortex or Thinking Brain................................24
   The Four Kinds of Brain Waves...................................26
   Show You Know 30

Overview of the 5 Steps of Accelerated Learning 32
   Show You Know 36

Step 1: Prepare Your State 37
   1) Get into Alpha State...38
   2) Listen to Classical Music (Baroque)......................41
   3) Create Specific Goals and Learning Objectives 42
   4) WII-FM – What's In It For Me?................................44
   5) Believe You Can Do It..46
   6) Prepare your Learning Space 49
   7) Manage your Physical and Mental Energy 52
   Show You Know 54

Step 2: Acquire the Skills and Knowledge...........................56
   The Big Picture 56
   Visual, Auditory, and Kinesthetic Learning Styles 59

Visual Strategies..62
Auditory Strategies..63
Kinesthetic Strategies 64
Multiple Intelligences...66
Show You Know 74

Step 3: Cement the Learning **76**
1) Make a Decision to Remember............................77
2) Association 79
3) Deliberately Create Multi-Sensory Memories....80
Memory Test Anyone?...82
4) Take Regular Breaks 84
5) Make the Information Stand Out........................86
6) Organize the Information Meaningfully..............88
7) Create a Mnemonic 89
8) Set it to Music..92
9) Memory Flashing 95
10) Sleep on it 96
11) Review the Material Frequently........................98
Show You Know 101

Step 4: Examine and Embrace **102**
Examine Your Knowledge 103
Embrace Your Knowledge 107
Show You Know 110

Step 5: Review, Revise, and Reward...................**111**
Review and Revise 111
Reward 113
Show You Know 117

Call to Action..**118**
Show You Know 120

Part 2: But Wait, There's More! Six Super Success Strategies

Introduction 122

Strategy #1: Take Effective Notes (Five Ninja Note-Taking Techniques) 124
Show You Know 132

Strategy #2: Read Faster (Five Simple Steps to Double Your Reading Speed) 133
Show You Know 138

Strategy #3: Set SMART Goals (Five Easy Strategies for Achieving SMART Goals) 139
Show You Know 148

Strategy #4: Manage Your Time (Ten Time-Management Tips for the Busy Student) 149
Show You Know 159

Strategy #5: Eat Healthy (Ten Brain-Healthy Foods for Smarter Eating) 160
Show You Know 164

Strategy #6: Be Happy (Ten Proven Ways to Increase Happiness) 166
Show You Know 175

Part 3: Closing Thoughts and Bonus Resources

Closing Thoughts 178

Bonus Resource 1: Top 20 Tips for Student Success............180

Bonus Resource 2: Killer Websites for Student Success......187

Bonus Resource 3: Calling All Callouts 192

Bonus Resource 4: Quoting All Quotes...................................196

Bibliography 203

About the Author...207

Acknowledgements

Nobody works in a vacuum. Most, if not all of life's great accomplishments, are achieved with the help and support of others. For me, writing this book was a great accomplishment; one that I had a lot of help and support with. I know you're excited to start learning faster, but I want to quickly thank the people who helped me finish the book you are about to enjoy.

First and foremost, let me thank my amazing wife Tara for her loving support, for her patience, and for her valuable input in editing all parts of this book. I also want to thank my daughter Aria for her super-duper cuteness and playful spirit. And I can't forget my dog Barkley – good boy. I want to thank my mom for her eagle eye in proofreading and Robin McFarland for her useful comments on the brain sections of this book. I also want to thank Tyler Oxford for his excellent coaching and Skye Gentile for our nightly check-ins. And finally, thank you to the many great artists over at www.fiverr.com. I used the talented folks at Fiverr to design my book cover, create most of the book's images, and format the book for publishing.

Introduction

"Success happens not by chance, but because you were given a chance and took advantage of it."

- Kevin Geary

Congratulations! The fact that you are reading this book means that you are a dedicated student who wants to be more successful in school and in life. It's said that 90% of success is just showing up, and that's exactly what you are doing right now. By reading this book, you are taking the first step toward academic mastery. I realize this is a bold claim, and yet I make it without any reservation whatsoever. The accelerated learning techniques presented in this book will allow you to learn more in less time. You will soon have the tools and the confidence to learn faster than ever before, **and** retain more of what you have learned. I hope you're as excited as I am!

From my experience, most high schools and colleges are not currently teaching the skills necessary to learn quickly and efficiently. To make matters worse, many teachers assume that you already know how to study effectively, and how to do well in their course. This is often not the case. Many students struggle not because they aren't smart, but because they have never been taught the skills and techniques presented in this book. Most students have never really been taught how to learn.

This is unfortunate because learning how to learn is one of the most valuable skills you can have. This is especially true in today's rapidly changing technological society. We have entered the information age where knowledge is king. To be successful, you need to be a lifelong learner. The days of having one career for your entire life are long gone. It has been estimated that the average person will hold more than seven different jobs after graduating college – many of them in completely different fields. Even if you are lucky enough to have the same career for your entire adult life, you will need to periodically upgrade your skills and knowledge in order to stay competitive. The faster and easier you can gain that knowledge, the more successful you will be.

Luckily, you are already an incredibly efficient learner. Consider all the things that you have learned outside of a formal classroom setting. You have learned how to walk, talk, swim, ride a bike, play various sports, drive a car, use a computer, cook a meal … the list goes on and on. Every one of these tasks is challenging and difficult, yet you are most likely extremely proficient at each.

Almost everything you have learned was through informal exploration. You learned through fun, play, conversation, and interaction with others. Informal learning is natural and fun, just ask any child. The problem is that formal classroom learning doesn't come naturally for many people. To make matters worse, most teachers have an unconscious tendency to teach using their preferred learning style (more on this later). If their preferred learning style doesn't match yours, there is a good chance you will find learning from them to be challenging.

Research shows that the current teaching methods used at many formal learning institutions such as high schools and universities do not effectively take into account how the brain works. According to Dr. John Medina, author of *Brain Rules*, "*If you wanted to create an educational environment that was directly opposed to what the brain was good at doing, you would probably design something like a classroom.*" As a result, classroom learning (in its present incarnation) usually only works well for a small number of students. For many people, their experience with formal learning has caused them to question their ability to learn at all. In one revealing study, 82% of children entering the school system at age 5 or 6 had a positive view of their ability to learn. By the time these children reached 16 years old, that positive rating had dropped dramatically to 18%!

If you have previously questioned your learning abilities, this book will change your mind. As stated previously, you are already an incredibly efficient learner. In fact, your brain is a supercomputer. Unfortunately, you were not given the instruction manual on how to efficiently use this incredible computer. Well, here it is! The information presented in this book will help you unlock the amazing potential of your brain.

As you will notice, this book is written in a casual, almost conversational tone, rather than the academic tone common in many textbooks. This was done on purpose. Even though I was a dedicated and serious student, I often struggled to read textbooks because of their overly dry presentation. I don't want that to be the case with this book. The information presented within these pages can literally change your life, and I want to make sure that you read all of it! My goal is that you truly enjoy reading this book. You may even find yourself staying home on a Friday or Saturday night because you just can't put it down. Ok, I admit that might be a little far fetched, but I do hope that you have fun while learning how you learn best.

You may also notice that this book doesn't have a lot of "filler" in it. I have made every attempt to make sure that everything contained within this book is essential and relevant to the task at hand – teaching you how to learn more efficiently. I know that you are busy, and I respect your time. Therefore, I made sure to keep this book short enough that you could read the entire thing in a few sittings. It wouldn't make a lot of sense to have a book about efficient learning strategies prattle on and on now would it?

As a final note, I wrote this book using the principles of accelerated learning. One of these principles is the frequent review of material that you want to commit to long-term memory. You will therefore see callouts like the one below interspersed throughout the book. These are used for key points that deserve special emphasis, so please pay attention to any callouts.

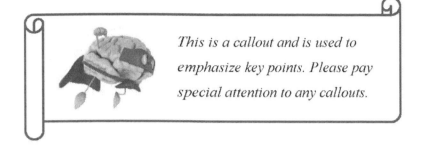

This is a callout and is used to emphasize key points. Please pay special attention to any callouts.

Another principle of accelerated learning is testing yourself to see how well you understand the material. At the end of each chapter is a brief *"Show You Know"* section with a few multiple-choice, true/false, fill-in-the-blank, or short-answer questions. These are designed to recall and test your understanding of the material presented in the chapter. Please do not skip these questions! Take the time to answer each one before you read the answers that follow. If you get them all correct, give yourself a pat on the back (literally – I mean it), and move on to the next chapter. If you get one or more wrong, please take the time to review the relevant sections before moving on.

What is that you say? Get on with it already!

Alright, without any further ado, let the adventure begin …

Part 1:
The Five Steps of
Accelerated Learning

Meet Your Amazing Brain

*"The brain is a monstrous, beautiful mess. Its billions of nerve cells -
called neurons - lie in a tangled web that displays cognitive powers
far exceeding any of the silicon machines we have built to mimic it."*
                                                    - William F. Allman

Before we jump right into accelerated learning techniques, let's
spend a few minutes exploring the most amazing and complex
computer ever created – your brain. Since accelerated learning
techniques are based upon how the brain processes, stores, and
recalls information, it will be a very beneficial exploration. This
chapter will provide you with background information that
will serve as a foundation for the learning techniques that
follow. It is not, by any means, meant to be a comprehensive
review of how the brain learns. My goal in writing this chapter
was to help you understand the WHY behind the techniques
you will soon be learning.

Let's start our exploration with a few basics. First, make a
fist with each hand. Now place them together with your
knuckles touching like you are giving yourself a knuckle bump.
This is a very rough estimate of the size of your brain, with
your fists representing the right and left hemispheres of your
brain. On average, an adult brain weighs approximately three
pounds. Although this is only about 2% of our body weight,
the brain consumes about 20% of our body's energy resources.
In other words, 20% of the calories we consume on a daily basis

go to keeping our brain working properly. This means that what we eat plays an important role in the overall health of our brain and how well it functions. (Brain-healthy foods will be discussed in a later chapter.)

The Triune Brain

The brain itself can actually be considered to be three brains in one, or "the triune brain" as described by neurologist Paul McLean. These three different parts of the brain evolved over time as we ourselves evolved and became human. The triune brain consists of the brain stem, the limbic system, and the neocortex, as shown in the figure on the next page. Let's take a quick look at the functions of each part of the triune brain. We'll focus our exploration on the functions that are most relevant to accelerated learning.

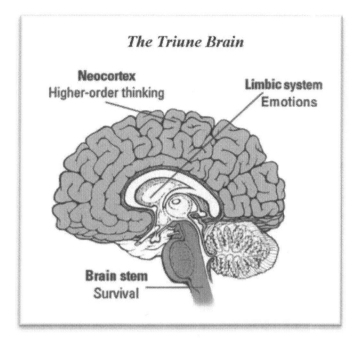

The Triune Brain

Neocortex
Higher-order thinking

Limbic system
Emotions

Brain stem
Survival

The Brain Stem or Reptilian Brain

The brain stem is located at the base of your skull. It is the part of the brain that we have in common with lower life forms such as reptiles, so it is also known as the reptilian brain. This is the part of the brain that is responsible for survival and basic vital life functions. The brain stem controls autonomic bodily functions, such as breathing, heart rate, and blood pressure. It also controls instinctive behavior, such as the fight or flight response. It is this aspect of the brain stem that is important to understand for learning.

Whenever we feel threatened or scared, our reptilian brain takes over, and we have very little access to our higher brain functions, such as reasoning and critical thinking. When our fight or flight response kicks in, adrenaline rushes through our body, and our brain downshifts into survival mode. We literally lose access to our higher order thinking skills. This mental downshifting is a survival strategy dating back to prehistoric times. If we saw a saber-toothed tiger out of the corner of our eye, the important thing was to take action rather than overanalyze the situation.

A better name for this behavior would actually be the freeze, flight, or fight response, because that is what we tend to do, in that order, when we sense a threat. First, we tend to freeze, then flee, and finally fight, if there are no other options. While this was a great strategy thousands of years ago, it's not so great now. As a student, it doesn't take a saber-toothed tiger to cause your freeze, flight, or fight response to kick in. Anytime we feel emotions such as fear, anxiety, stress, or threat, this response kicks in to some degree and our higher-order thinking skills become impaired.

If you have ever gone blank during a quiz or exam, it is most likely because you became anxious or stressed for some reason and then literally could not think clearly. You knew the answer to the question or how to do the problem, but you couldn't access the information at the time. Don't you hate it when that happens? Well, don't worry because you will soon have an awesome technique to use in that situation. One of the very first steps of accelerated learning is getting in the optimal mental state for learning, a brain-wave state in which you have maximum access to your higher-order thinking. More on that later.

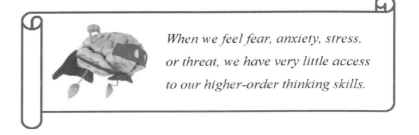

When we feel fear, anxiety, stress, or threat, we have very little access to our higher-order thinking skills.

The Limbic System or Mammalian Brain

The limbic system is the part of the brain that we have in common with other mammals, which is why it is sometimes called the mammalian brain. It is responsible for more complex brain functions such as regulation of the immune and hormone systems, sexuality, mood, feelings, and emotions. The limbic system also controls an important part of our long-term memory storage. The parts of the limbic system that are relevant for understanding accelerated learning are the thalamus, the amygdala, and the hippocampus.

The thalamus acts like a kind of switchboard for our brain. All of the visual, auditory, and kinesthetic information from our senses enters the thalamus, where it is categorized and sent to different parts of the brain for processing. The thalamus actually sends sensory information in two different directions at the same time. The first direction (the high road) leads to the sensory cortices: the visual cortex, the auditory cortex, and the somatosensory cortex. These are located in the neocortex and will be discussed in more detail in the next section. As shown in the figure below, the second direction in which the thalamus sends sensory information (the low road) leads to the amygdala.

The Path of Learning and Memory

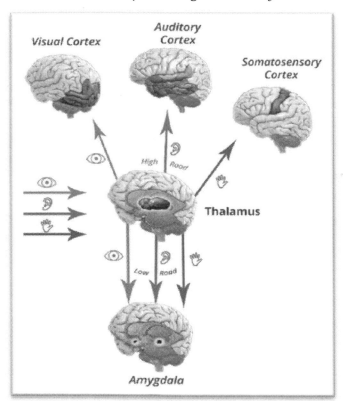

Image inspired by www.quantumlearning.com.

The amygdala is our emotional control center. One of its jobs is to analyze incoming information for emotional significance and determine if it should initiate a freeze, flight, or fight response. It is the amygdala that is responsible for the mental downshifting that happens when the reptilian brain takes over. Anytime your amygdala senses emotions such as fear, anxiety, stress, or threat (which can be remembered with the acronym FAST), it quickly sends a signal to your brain stem. Your brain stem then activates your freeze, flight or fight response and your higher-order thinking skills literally go out the window. Goodbye learning, hello panic. Learning is virtually impossible in this state. Positive emotions such as joy, fun, and excitement are, therefore, extremely important to the learning process.

The hippocampus is located below the thalamus near the middle of our brain. As with the thalamus and the amygdala, we have one in each cerebral hemisphere. The hippocampus is the memory control center of the brain. It is responsible for storing short-term memories, deciding which short-term memories get encoded into long-term memory, and sending those memories to the appropriate sensory cortices for long-term storage. The hippocampus is also responsible for retrieving those long-term memories when they are needed.

The fact that the limbic system controls both emotions and long-term memory storage has an important implication for learning. Things that involve strong emotions are very well remembered. You can think of emotions almost like post-it notes that tell our brain to pay attention and remember this information. One of the jobs of the amygdala is to attach these emotional post-it notes to memories. The stronger the emotion, the stronger the memory. This is why emotionally rich events, that occurred many years ago, are remembered in much greater detail than mundane events that happened recently. For example, you probably remember your first kiss more vividly than what you had for dinner a month ago. The more positive emotion you can attach to a memory, the stronger it will be stored and the more likely you will be to remember it. Since learning a new subject is, in essence, creating memories of new knowledge and skills, incorporating positive emotions into the learning process can do wonders for your academic success.

Positive emotions such as fun, joy, and excitement are important for both learning and memory.

The Neocortex or Thinking Brain

The neocortex, or thinking brain, is the part of the brain that makes us most human. It is the home of all our higher intelligences. It is responsible for critical thinking, reasoning, language, and our ability to conceive abstractly. The neocortex itself is divided into separate areas (lobes) for speech, vision, hearing, and touch. The parts of the neocortex that will be useful to understand for your journey toward academic mastery are shown in the figure below. These are the visual cortex, the auditory cortex, and the somatosensory cortex.

The Path of Learning and Memory / Prefrontal Cortex

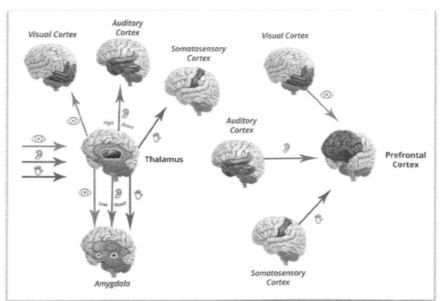

Image inspired by www.quantumlearning.com.

Recall from the above figure that information from our senses gets sent along the high road to the sensory cortices (while at the same time being sent along the low road to the amygdala). Everything that we see, all of the information we receive through our eyes, gets sent to our visual cortex. If you take one of your hands and place it on the back of your head, your hand will be directly above your visual cortex. Everything that we hear, all of the information we receive through our ears, gets sent to our auditory cortex. If you cup your hands over your ears, this is approximately where your auditory cortex is located on each side of your brain. And finally, everything that we do with our bodies, all of the information we receive through our tactile senses such as temperature, texture, body position, and pain, gets sent to our somatosensory cortex. If you run one of your hands from ear to ear over the top of your head, your hand will trace out the approximate position of your somatosensory cortex.

Our visual, auditory, and somatosensory cortices then process the information they receive from the thalamus and send it on to our prefrontal cortex, which is the home of our working memory. From there things get complicated. To make a long story short, if the information gets flagged for long-term memory, it eventually returns to the same sensory cortex that processed it for long-term storage. This means that visual memories are stored separately in the visual cortex, auditory memories in the auditory cortex, and kinesthetic memories in the somatosensory cortex. The fact that different kinds of memories are stored in different parts of the brain means that anything we learn will be stored more deeply if we learn it using multiple senses. (Note: I have not discussed our senses of taste and smell, because these are not usually associated with learning.)

We create stronger and more permanent memories when we store the information using all of our senses.

The Four Kinds of Brain Waves

The nerve cells in the brain that are responsible for thinking, and that are allowing you to read this fascinating book, are called neurons. Each of us has about the same number of neurons – around 100 billion (recent studies suggest about 86 billion). The neurons in our brain connect to other neurons in vast, complex networks. Each neuron can connect with up to 20,000 other neurons. With almost 100 billion neurons, each connecting with up to 20,000 other neurons, the number of possible connections is staggering. According to Robert Ornstein and Richard Thompson in *The Amazing Brain*, "*the number of possible interconnections between these cells is greater than the number of atoms in the universe*".

These billions of neurons form huge networks of neural connections and communicate with each other through electrical signals. In essence, very tiny currents of electricity are sent between neurons. These electric currents are sometimes called brain waves because of their cyclic wavelike nature (see image below).

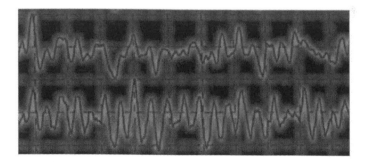

Brain waves can be measured using an electroencephalograph (EEG), which uses hundreds of electrodes to measure the frequency of brain waves in cycles per second or Hertz (Hz). The results of EEG studies show that there are four main kinds of brain waves: delta, theta, alpha, and beta, and these brain waves are strongly correlated with our state of mind.

Delta

Delta waves (~0.1 – 4 Hz) are the slowest of the four brain waves and are associated with deep, dreamless sleep. It is when the brain is in delta state that the body repairs itself.

Theta

Theta brain waves are faster than delta and have a frequency of about 4 – 7 Hz. Theta state is associated with the early stages of sleep and deep meditation. Memories are processed and stored when our brains are in theta state. This is why a good night's sleep is so important. Memory formation and learning depend upon it.

Beta

Beta brain waves (~13-30 Hz) are the fastest and are associated with normal alert consciousness. This is the state in which we spend most of our lives. When we are in beta state, our brain is constantly changing focus from one thing to another. This is great for things like driving or parenting, where you have many different things to focus on. However, beta state is not the best state to be in for learning. That state is alpha state.

Alpha

Alpha brain waves have a frequency around 7 – 13 Hz and are associated with being awake and alert but relaxed. When we are in alpha state, our brain is functioning most efficiently. We can harness our brain's full resources and focus deeply on one thing. Athletes and performers who are in the "zone" are operating in alpha state. As a student, alpha state is the Holy Grail for learning. If you want to learn most effectively, you want your brain to be in alpha state. It is **the optimal state** to be in for learning.

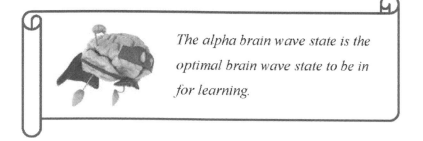

The alpha brain wave state is the optimal brain wave state to be in for learning.

So that's it – everything I think you need to know about the brain to get you started and help you understand why the techniques you will soon be learning are so effective. There will also be additional brain information interspersed throughout this book so stay tuned. If you want more detailed information about the brain and how we learn, I highly recommend reading the informative and entertaining *Brain Rules* by Dr. John Medina. You can also check out the bibliography at the end of this book for other brain-related books.

Before you move on to the next chapter, please make sure to read and answer all of the "Show You Know" questions. It won't take very long, and it will help your understanding and recall of this valuable information.

Show You Know

1) The triune brain consists of the brain stem, the limbic system, and the _____.

2) What part of the brain is responsible for the mental downshifting that occurs when the reptilian brain takes over?

3) All types of memories (visual, auditory, and kinesthetic) are stored in the same place in the brain. True or False?

4) The optimal brain-wave state to be in for learning is:

a) Alpha.
b) Beta.
c) Theta.
d) Delta.

Answers:

1) Neocortex or thinking brain.
2) The amygdala.
3) False. Long-term memories are stored in the same sensory cortex that originally processed the information (visual information in the visual cortex ...).
4) Alpha state.

Overview of the 5 Steps of Accelerated Learning

"Live as if you were to die tomorrow. Learn as if you were to live forever."

– Mahatma Gandhi

Now that we know a bit about how our brains work, let's take a quick look at how accelerated learning techniques take advantage of this information to optimize learning. The purpose of this chapter is to give our brain the big picture of the five steps of accelerated learning. Then we will look at each of the steps in greater detail.

1) Prepare Your State (Mental, Emotional, and Physical)

The most important thing you can do before starting any task or project is to adopt a positive and resourceful state. This is especially true of learning. If you begin a learning project or study session with a negative mental, emotional, or physical state, you are practically setting yourself up for failure. The first step of accelerated learning is to deliberately create a positive, confident, and resourceful state. Since our mental, emotional, and physical states are all connected, this can be easily accomplished using a few simple techniques designed to change each of our three states.

2) Acquire the Skills and Knowledge

After deliberately creating an optimal state for learning, we are now ready to acquire new skills and knowledge. This begins with the big picture of what we will be learning. Before we tackle a new subject, we want to start with an overview of how everything fits together. This gives our brain a framework in which to assemble the new information into a cohesive and unified picture. We can then concentrate on using our preferred learning style(s) and intelligence(s) to learn as efficiently as possible.

Research performed by experts in Neuro-Linguistic Programming (or NLP) has identified three distinct learning and communication styles: visual, auditory, and kinesthetic. Although we use all three learning styles when taking in new information, people generally prefer one learning style over the other two. When we process information using our preferred learning style, we tend to learn it faster and easier. In the second step of accelerated learning, we acquire the information and skills using the learning style or styles that work best for us.

We then want to explore what we have just learned using our multiple intelligences. In order to really learn something and commit it to long-term memory, we must turn mere facts into meaning. We want to thoroughly explore the subject matter. Our goal is to interpret the information and make it personal and meaningful. The more meaningful we can make the information, the faster and easier we will learn it.

3) Cement the Learning

Learning something new does us no good if we can't remember it and put it to use. You have probably heard the expression "use it or lose it". This is especially true of our brains. If we don't use what we've just learned in some way, our brains will delete it to make room for new information that may be more useful to us. In fact, studies suggest that up to 80% of what we learn will be forgotten within 24 hours unless some special effort is made to remember it. We want to make sure that this does not happen. In this third step of accelerated learning, we make sure that newly-learned information is firmly planted into our long-term memory. We do that by making a deliberate effort to remember by using a variety of simple and practical memory techniques.

4) Examine and Embrace

In the fourth step of accelerated learning, you demonstrate exactly what you have learned to yourself and to others. You examine your knowledge and test your understanding of the material. The goal is to see how well you understand the information and determine if there are any gaps in your knowledge.

Once you are satisfied that you know the material, you need to take that knowledge and apply it. It is one thing to learn something, but it is another thing to actually use what you have just learned. By embracing the knowledge, you are taking it out of the theoretical realm and into the practical. You are showing that the knowledge is now yours and you own it!

5) Review, Revise, and Reward

The final step of accclerated learning is to review the entire learning process. The purpose is to reflect not on **what** you have learned, but on **how** you have learned. We review how we learned so we can improve the process the next time around. Learning how you learn best is an ongoing process that takes practice and revision. We continually revise our learning process until we find the techniques and strategies that work best for us.

And last, but certainly not least, we celebrate! We want to reward our efforts, so we train our brain to associate pleasure with learning. The reward can be as simple as calling a friend to share our successes, or as elaborate as a weekend getaway.

The five steps of the accelerated learning process can be remembered with the acronym **PACER**: **P**repare your state, **A**cquire the skills and knowledge, **C**ement the learning, **E**xamine and embrace, and **R**eview, revise, and reward.

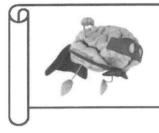

*The 5 steps of accelerated learning can be remembered with the acronym **PACER**.*

Show You Know

1) What does the acronym PACER stand for?

2) I'm excited to know how to double my learning (it's on the next page). True or False?

Answers:

1) **P**repare your state, **A**cquire the skills and knowledge, **C**ement the learning, **E**xamine and embrace, **R**eview, revise, and reward.
2) True. (At least I hope so!)

Step 1: Prepare Your State

The first step of accelerated learning, one which is almost always overlooked, is getting into the right state – mentally, emotionally, and physically. From my experience, most students don't consider their mental or emotional state before studying. They just sit down and study, even if they're worried, anxious, or stressed. As you can imagine, most of these students only achieve a small fraction of what they are capable of achieving.

As all top athletes know, getting into the right state before an athletic event is extremely important. The same is true for learning. In fact, spending just 5 to 10 minutes preparing your mental, emotional, and physical state before learning is perhaps the single most important thing you can do. This alone can double your learning, even if you implement none of the other steps of accelerated learning. Let me say that again. Spending just 5 to 10 minutes preparing your state can double your learning. Pretty sweet, huh?

So how do you prepare to learn? It's actually quite easy. Outlined below are seven techniques that you can use before you begin studying to make sure that you're in the optimal mental, emotional, and physical states for learning.

We can double our learning by spending just 5 – 10 minutes preparing our state.

1) Get into Alpha State

As we learned earlier during our exploration of the brain, our higher brain functions, such as reasoning and logical thinking, are virtually shut down if we are experiencing stress and physical or emotional danger. In general, any negative emotions will inhibit our learning. The ideal mental state for learning is a relaxed, confident and resourceful state of mind, corresponding to the alpha brain-wave state.

There are many different techniques you can use to get into a relaxed and resourceful state of mind. Before every quiz or exam, I lead my college physics classes through the eight step process described below. I first learned the process from an amazing company called Quantum Learning and then modified it for my college students. It's quick, easy to do, and extremely effective.

Alpha State Process:

1) Say "shift into alpha state" - either silently or out loud. (Note: this is a cueing phrase that can be changed. See notes below.)
2) Sit up straight.
3) Allow a deep breath in.
4) Close your eyes as you exhale quietly.
5) Keep your eyes closed as you continue to allow slow, deep breaths.
6) Picture in your mind's eye a peaceful place, where you feel calm, confident, relaxed, resourceful, and at ease.
7) Allow the image to become brighter and more vibrant. See the scene through your own eyes, and hear the sounds through your own ears.
8) With your eyes still closed, look straight up, and look back down; open your eyes and focus.

This process allows us to quickly shift into alpha state because our mental, emotional, and physical states are all connected. Each step in the alpha state process is designed to shift one of the three states, which also affects the other two. For example, sitting up straight will shift your physical state into a more confident one. This then has a positive effect on both your mental and emotional states.

Here are two quick notes about steps 1 and 6:

1) The cueing phrase can be anything you want. It is a phrase that you say to yourself, either out loud or internally, every time you begin the process. Eventually, your brain will associate the phrase with being in alpha state, and the two will become anchored together. Once that happens, simply saying the phrase can cause your brain to shift into a more alpha-like brain-wave state.

6) Your peaceful place is somewhere, real or imaginary, where you feel calm, relaxed, peaceful, and safe. It is someplace where you feel self-assured and confident, where you feel like you are at your best. It might be your home or bedroom, a church or synagogue, the beach, a favorite vacation spot – anyplace you want. Once you have the place in mind, really try and imagine yourself there. Visualize what you would see, hear, feel, and smell.

The more you do this process, the easier and more automatic the steps will become. As a student, I recommend getting into alpha state right before class starts, before studying, and especially before taking any quiz or exam. During an exam, if you ever find yourself panicking and your mind goes blank, you can quickly do this process to get back into a more resourceful state of mind.

The alpha brain wave state is the optimal brain wave state to be in for learning. Yes, I said it again!

2) Listen to Classical Music (Baroque)

As you probably know, music can have a tremendous effect on how we feel and on our energy level. In fact, music is often used to create a desired mood. It can be used to pump us up while working out, help us relax after a long day, or even bring back pleasant memories. Music can also be used to help us focus and study.

In addition to the alpha state process described above, another way to induce a relaxed and resourceful state of mind is through the use of classical music – more specifically, Baroque music. Baroque is a specific genre of classical music composed between ~1600 and 1750. It has about 50 to 80 beats per minute, which matches a normal resting heart rate. Various studies have shown that listening to Baroque music can have a positive impact on your ability to learn and retain information. It also helps to promote a feeling of calmness and relaxation that is beneficial to learning.

Some composers from the Baroque era include:

- Johann Sebastian Bach
- George Frideric Handel
- Antonio Vivaldi
- Georg Philipp Telemann
- Arcangelo Corelli
- Henry Purcell
- Johann Pachelbel Rameau

When using Baroque music to enhance your studying, you should listen to it at low volume. Ideally, you want the music to be background noise, so that it's barely audible. You want your brain to be focusing on your work, not on the music that you're playing.

3) Create Specific Goals and Learning Objectives

Before you sit down to study, it is important to spend a minute or two thinking about exactly what you want to get out of the study session. You want to start with a clear vision of what you want to accomplish. If you do not have a clear goal, chances are good that you won't accomplish what you need to get done. Think about it this way ... it is extremely difficult to hit a target that you can't see.

Your learning goal should be a specific and measurable target. A goal such as, "I will study math for a while", is vague and unclear. Exactly how long is a while? Ideally, a specific goal includes a number or quantity. For example, a better math goal would be: "I will read 15 pages in my math textbook and then finish five homework problems." The more specific your goal, the more likely you'll be to accomplish it. See Part 2 of this book for a set of simple strategies for setting and achieving SMART goals.

In addition to being specific, your goal should be objective-based, not time-based. If your goal is to study science for 45 minutes, it is easy to sit down and seem busy for 45 minutes, without really accomplishing anything. It is much better to specify an objective such as "read Chapter 2 of the text book, take notes on the reading, and then finish the first 4 homework problems".

Once you have accomplished your learning goal, take a few moments to celebrate your success. Choose a specific reward for completing your goal. The reward can be as simple as calling a friend, watching a favorite TV show, having a tasty dessert, or even going for a walk. Whatever it is, get into the habit of noticing and celebrating your successes – especially those around learning. This will anchor positive emotions to setting and achieving your learning goals.

4) WII-FM – What's In It For Me?

Believe it or not, I know what your favorite radio station is. How can I possibly know that? Because everyone loves the same station: WII-FM. OK, this isn't an actual radio station. It is an acronym that stands for the following question: **What's In It For Me?**

The answer to this simple question will have a profound impact on your motivation to learn, which, in turn, will greatly impact your actual learning.

People are rarely motivated to do something that they don't see as relevant to their own lives. This is also true of studying and learning a new subject. It you can't see the personal relevance of a class, you will not be motivated to study or put in the effort necessary to succeed. On the other hand, when you can see the personal benefits, your motivation and desire to succeed will be greatly enhanced.

Many of the most successful people on the planet are just ordinary people who are extraordinarily motivated. Why are they so motivated? Because they have figured out what's in it for them. In other words, they know their WHY! Do you want to be more motivated toward your classes and enjoy them more? If so, then it is absolutely vital that you figure out your WHY. The more compelling the reason why you want something, the easier it will be to figure out how to get it. Or said another way, the bigger your WHY, the easier your HOW.

You can train yourself to be motivated and see the WHY behind every class by focusing on the positive impact of your learning. You can ask yourself questions such as:

- *"Why is this subject important?"*
- *"Why do I need to learn this?"*
- *"How can I use this information in my everyday life?"*
- *"How will learning this improve my life?"*
- *"What are some of the advantages of learning this?"*

Now, I understand that staying motivated for certain classes can sometimes be challenging. Seeing the personal benefits is often easier said than done. You may have to take required classes that you really don't want to take. If and when that happens, my best advice is to try and see the big picture. Each class is a stepping stone to your future. In order to graduate and get one step closer to your dream job, you need to pass your classes – all of them. Do whatever you can to see the WHY behind each of your classes. Three of the most important ingredients for success as a student are motivation, motivation, and motivation!

The bigger your WHY, the easier your HOW!

5) Believe You Can Do It

"It is our attitude at the beginning of a difficult task which, more than anything else, will affect its successful outcome."

–William James

Do you want to know one of the keys to dramatically increasing you chances of achieving any goal or quickly learning any new skill? Of course you do! Who wouldn't? Well, here it is. One of the keys to succeeding in anything is simply the belief that you can and will succeed. To paraphrase a famous quote by Henry Ford: *"Whether you think you can, or whether you think you can't, either way, you are usually right."* Your chances for success are dramatically increased if you simply believe that you will succeed. This is especially true of learning. One of the best things you can do as a student is to foster a strong belief in yourself and your ability to learn.

Regardless of how well you may have done in the past, every single person reading this book has the ability to achieve more in less time. We are all born with the same number of neurons; it is what you do with your neurons that counts. Numerous studies have shown that the majority of a student's success depends not on their IQ or technical ability, but on effective learning techniques. The techniques and strategies presented in this book will allow you to get the most out of your 86 billion neurons.

One way that you can develop your belief in yourself is through the use of positive affirmations. Some examples of positive affirmations include:

- *"I learn anything easily and effortlessly."*
- *"I always get better with practice."*
- *"I love to learn."*
- *"My brain is powerful and capable of learning anything."*

You can say positive affirmations out loud or silently to yourself. When using affirmations, be present with what you are saying, and try to embody the statement. The goal is to feel what you are saying and not just repeat the words mindlessly. I also recommend placing positive affirmations around your work area or study space. I sometimes put affirmations or quotes on post-it notes and hang them on my computer monitor as reminders. I believe that daily exposure to positive messages has a beneficial effect on my attitude toward learning and toward life.

Other ways that you can develop your belief in yourself and your ability to learn include:

- Visualize your success.
- Keep a success journal.
- Read something inspiring every day.
- Eat healthy and exercise regularly.
- Get a good night's sleep.
- Replace self-limiting thoughts with positive ones.
- Reduce your exposure to television and other sources of negative media.
- Associate with positive people.

"Believe in yourself, and the rest will fall into place. Have faith in your own abilities, work hard, and there is nothing you cannot accomplish."

– Brad Henry

6) Prepare your Learning Space

Now that you know how to prepare your mind for learning, let's take a look at preparing an optimal learning space. Where you study may not seem like a big deal, but it can actually have a significant effect on how well you learn. A poor study environment can negatively impact student success and undermine even the best learning strategies. The following are several things to consider when designing an optimal learning space.

Location:

Your learning space should be a place that is free from distractions – someplace used just for studying. This will create an association in your subconscious mind between your learning space and studying. You want your brain to know that every time you sit down at your learning space, you are there to work and you mean business. Contrast this to studying at the kitchen table, a place that most of us associate with eating. My guess is that if you sit at your kitchen table to study, you often snack while studying. Am I right? Similarly, the association between our beds and sleep often makes it difficult to read or study in bed without feeling tired.

Lighting:

We have a basic human need for natural light. In fact, the decreased amount of light in winter months can lead to a form of depression in some people called Seasonal Affective

Disorder, which is often treated with light therapy. Whenever possible, choose natural light over artificial light. Ideally, your learning space should have large windows that allow plenty of natural light. When you must use artificial light, incandescent light is better than fluorescent light (energy considerations aside). Place the lamp so the light is uniform and does not cause glare. This will reduce eye strain and improve your overall productivity.

Plants:

As humans, our brains are hard-wired to respond positively to natural elements in our environment that we find nurturing. Studies have shown that work performed under the calming influence of nature is more accurate than work done in an environment devoid of natural elements. Placing a plant or two on or around your desk can help create a calming environment and have a positive impact on your learning. If you do not have a green thumb, you can always use a fake plant. While these can be expensive, I have had good luck finding nice, inexpensive fake plants at thrift stores such as Goodwill.

Organization:

It should go without saying ... the more organized your learning space, the better. Place frequently used items, such as paper, pencils, erasers, books, highlighters, calculators and index cards, so they are within easy reach. Every time you need to stop studying in order to get up and retrieve one of these items, it will take your brain a little bit of time to get back on track. This will decrease your overall efficiency and make it less likely that you will recall the information at a later time.

Other things to consider are:

Availability:

Your learning space should be available to you whenever you need it. If it is not, you will need to have at least one alternate learning space.

Temperature:

Your learning space should be a comfortable temperature – not too hot or too cold.

Music:

You should have access to music or any other audible stimuli that you need for learning. As discussed above, playing Baroque music at low volume can be very effective for studying.

Ergonomics:

You want a comfortable chair with a good back that you can sit in comfortably for at least 45 minutes. A chair with arms will allow you to rest your elbows and keep your wrists straight while typing. This also requires that your keyboard is at the right height. In addition, your computer monitor should be at head height and about a foot away from you. Finally, you want your desk to be at a comfortable height for writing (and typing if your keyboard sits on your desk).

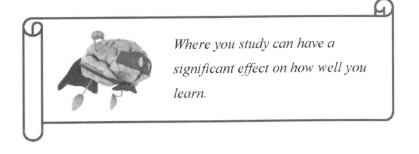

Where you study can have a significant effect on how well you learn.

7) Manage your Physical and Mental Energy

As a student, one of the most important skills you can have, one that will help you succeed in school and in life, is the ability to manage your physical and mental energy. Managing your energy is all about being aware of how you are feeling - both physically and mentally. Have you ever tried to study while you were physically tired or mentally exhausted? I have, and it is not easy. In fact, it is virtually impossible to study effectively if you can barely keep your eyes open. It is much better to take a 10-minute break and do something energizing, than trying to plow forward in an exhausted state. Here are a few ideas for quick energy-boosting breaks:

- Go for a walk around the block.
- Put on an upbeat song and move your body.
- Get a glass of water and a light snack.

- Spend 5 to 10 minutes doing jumping jacks, sit-ups, push-ups, or any other exercise.
- Make a cup of green tea.
- Take a 15-minute power nap.

Managing your physical and mental energy also includes knowing when, during the day, you are at your best. In other words, when is the best time of day for you to study? Only you can answer that question. Some people are most productive in the morning, other people in the afternoon or at night. *When are you most productive? When do you find it easiest to study? Are you more focused in the morning or at night?* These are important questions to ask. If you really want to be more productive and learn faster, then you absolutely must know when you learn best.

For me, I learned the hard way while writing this book that I am no good at creative writing late in the afternoon or immediately after dinner. I am more focused and creative right when I first get up or between 9 pm and midnight. Because of this, I now make sure that I write in the morning or late at night. If I must work in the afternoon or after dinner, I make sure I do busy work, such as organizing papers.

Similarly, you should schedule your studying for those times when you are most focused. If you know that you are most productive and focused in the evenings, make sure you arrange your schedule so you have the evening free for studying. This will not only allow you to learn more efficiently, it will also increase your ability to recall the material when you need it later.

"I don't care how much power, brilliance or energy you have, if you don't harness it and focus it on a specific target, and hold it there you're never going to accomplish as much as your ability warrants."

–Zig Ziglar

Show You Know

1) Spending just 5 – 10 minutes preparing your mental, emotional, and physical states can double your learning. True or False?

2) What genre of music can be used to induce a relaxed and resourceful state of mind?

3) What is everyone's favorite radio station?

4) When are you the most productive and focused?

   a) In the morning.
   b) In the afternoon.
   c) In the evening.

Answers:

1) True.

2) Baroque.

3) WII-FM (What's In It For Me).

4) Only you can answer this question. Schedule your studying for those times when you are most productive and focused.

Step 2: Acquire the Skills and Knowledge

"How you study is WAY more important than how much you study."

– Dr. Joe McCullough

After you have gotten into the optimal mental, emotional, and physical state for learning, the next step is to acquire your new skills and knowledge. This begins with getting an overview or big picture of what you will be learning. Most students vastly underestimate the importance of starting with the big picture. Most students also spend way more time studying than they need to.

The Big Picture

Learning a new subject or skill is like doing a 1000-piece jigsaw puzzle. Imagine trying to do the puzzle without knowing how it is supposed to look. You don't know how the pieces should fit together, because you lost the top of the box the puzzle came in! Can you muscle through and eventually finish the mystery puzzle? Of course you can! Is it going to be a lot harder and take more time than if you knew what the puzzle should look like? Of course it will!

The exact same thing is true for learning any new skill or subject. If you enter blindly, without any knowledge of how everything fits together, you are setting yourself up for wasted time and effort. You are basically trying to do a puzzle without any idea of what it should look like. Knowing the big picture gives your brain a framework in which to place the puzzle pieces of new knowledge. Starting with the big picture not only makes the learning process more efficient, it also increases recall of the information at a later time.

Starting with the big picture makes the learning process more efficient and increases recall.

So how exactly do you get the big picture? By simply spending time browsing through the material you will be learning. For example, before you start a new class, make sure that you read the syllabus and spend time browsing through the course materials (textbook, course web site, hand outs ...). As you browse through everything, really try to think about, and imagine the personal relevance of the material. In addition to getting an overview of what you will be learning, it will motivate your brain by giving it the all important WHY. (Remember your favorite station: WII-FM?)

One of the best "big picture" strategies you can adopt as a student is to preview the material you will be learning – before attending class. If at all possible, I recommend spending 10 to 15 minutes immediately before class previewing the material. Scheduling may make that impossible, so be flexible. Previewing the night before is much better than not at all.

If your class has an assigned textbook, your preview can simply be reading the relevant sections of the book. You can also take advantage of the numerous free educational resources available online. Thousands of instructors have their course material (lecture notes, PowerPoint slides, old exams ...) posted online and freely available to all. In addition, web sites such as YouTube and MIT OpenCourseWare have outstanding videos – covering almost every imaginable topic. Just keep in mind when using online resources that anyone can post anything online, even if it is not correct. To illustrate this point, I sometimes show my students YouTube videos on "free energy" and "perpetual motion machines" (neither of which is possible) that sound very convincing and plausible to the uninformed. I also remind them that Wikipedia is not the final authority! If you do use online resources, please make sure that you find a reliable source that you trust.

Previewing the material you'll be learning also applies to reading, especially when doing assigned reading for a class. If you are reading a chapter in the textbook, take a couple of minutes to skim through the chapter before you start reading.

Make a mental note of chapter headings, bolded text, pictures, and other information that stands out on the page. Your goal is to give your brain the big picture of what you will be learning, an overview of the entire chapter. This is like looking at a picture of the completed puzzle before you start to assemble the pieces.

If you have questions to answer for a reading assignment, read them first. When you come across the answers, they will literally jump off the page at you. If you have your own questions about the material, take a moment to write them down. Your brain will then be alert for information that answers those questions.

Visual, Auditory, and Kinesthetic Learning Styles

Now that you've given your brain the big picture of what you will be learning, it's time to get down to business and acquire your new skills and knowledge. To do that, you are going to take advantage of the different learning styles. There are three primary ways our brains acquire, process, and learn new information: visually (what we see), auditorily (what we hear) and kinesthetically (what we do). These different learning modalities correspond to the three primary learning styles: visual, auditory, and kinesthetic (VAK), which are described below.

Visual learners learn best through seeing. They enjoy pictures, diagrams, demonstrations, and watching videos. Visual learners tend to be strong readers, good spellers, and pay close attention to a speaker's body language and facial expressions. They find it easier to remember things they see than things they hear. They are generally not distracted by noise, tend to like art more than music, prefer reading for themselves rather than being read to, and tend to memorize by visual association.

Auditory learners learn best through hearing. They enjoy audio tapes, discussions, and verbal instructions. They would rather listen to material presented in lecture than read the material in a textbook. Auditory learners tend to prefer talking to writing and are often easily distracted by noise. They find it easier to remember things they hear than things they see. Auditory learners usually enjoy reading aloud, tend to move their lips while reading, tend to like music more than art, and are frequently eloquent speakers.

Kinesthetic learners learn best by doing. They enjoy manipulating, moving, touching, and hands-on experiences where they can be directly involved. They learn best through movement and physical activities and understand things better when they act them out. Kinesthetic learners tend to speak and write more slowly, stand close when talking to someone, and touch people to get their attention. They find it easier to remember things when they are being physically active.

Kinesthetic learner are usually good at sports, tend to gesture a lot while talking, tend to use action words, and often can't sit still for long periods of time.

Although everyone uses all three learning styles, most people generally prefer one over the other two. When you learn using your preferred learning style, you tend to learn more effectively, and with the least amount of effort. So which style do you prefer? My guess is that you already have a good idea about your preferred learning style from the previous descriptions. If not, there are numerous free tests available online to help you determine your preferred learning style. You can find them by doing a Google search for "VAK learning styles test".

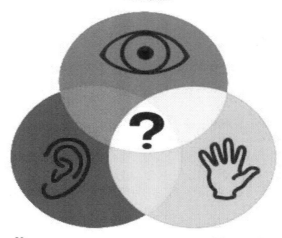

Visual

Auditory

Kinesthetic

What kind of learner are you?

Once you know your preferred learning style(s), you can align your study habits to best match your style. This is important because you can't choose how material is presented to you during class. However, you can choose how to study and review the information on your own. When you study and learn using your preferred style, you learn faster and remember more. And that is what this book is all about now, isn't it?

Listed below are techniques that can be used for each of the three different learning styles. As you read through them, choose a few techniques from each learning style that resonate with you.

Visual Strategies

The best visual learning strategy, and in fact, one of the most useful of all learning techniques, is the use of a learning map. Learning maps, also known as mind maps, were created by Tony Buzzan. A learning map is a visual representation of a subject where the connections between different topics can be easily seen.

To create a learning map, start with the main topic centered in the middle of the page (turn the page horizontally to maximize space). Topics are represented using keywords, phrases, and/or pictures. Branch out from the center for each key point, connecting related topics to the main one. You can build out from each branch to add additional details. As you create branches and sub-branches, underline words and use bold letters. Use symbols, bright colors, pictures, and other images to make important words jump off the page. Be creative and develop your own style. The more you practice using mind maps, the better you will get at creating them. The mind maps you have created will then serve as excellent tools for reviewing and/or studying.

Here are some additional strategies for visual learners:

- Sit where you have a clear view of your teacher when they are speaking.
- Take detailed notes using lots of color; develop your own color coding.
- Use a highlighter while reading.
- Review the pictures and diagrams from your textbook.
- Summarize material using charts, graphs and diagrams.
- Use multimedia such as computer animations and videos.
- Visualize and create a mental picture of what you are learning.

Auditory Strategies

One of the best learning strategies, in general, is cooperative learning. This is especially useful for auditory learners. Find a study buddy or study group with whom you can discuss your ideas and share what you are learning. Take turns explaining the material to each other. If you can't explain what you have learned to someone else, you don't really understand it. After you have finished learning a topic, quiz each other to review the material. In addition to being a useful learning strategy, studying with another person is often more enjoyable.

Some additional strategies for auditory learners include:

- Ask a lot of questions during class.
- Actively participate in all class discussions.
- Study in a quiet place away from verbal distractions.
- Create musical jingles and mnemonics when memorizing material.
- Read material out loud (the more dramatic the better).
- Use a tape recorder to summarize your notes and listen to them in the car.

Kinesthetic Strategies

The key for kinesthetic learners is active, physical involvement during the learning process. Some learning strategies that kinesthetic learners can incorporate include:

- Take notes in class – then rewrite your notes.
- Read the textbook.

- Put a checkmark at the end of each paragraph or page to show that you understand the material.
- Make notes on index cards or post-its and arrange in a logical sequence.
- Walk around while you read or listen to audio tapes.
- Shift your position while sitting.
- Take frequent study breaks.
- Create motions or gestures to help remember content.
- Chew gum while studying.

Experiment with these different strategies and techniques. See which ones work best for you, which ones you enjoy the most. As a general rule, you should use a combination of techniques when learning any subject. Because our brain stores visual, auditory, and kinesthetic information in different places, the more senses we use, the better the information will be stored in our long-term memory.

"You don't understand anything until you learn it more than one way."

– Marvin Minsky

Ideally, you want to use strategies from each learning style whenever you study. Combining techniques can be as simple as reading and visualizing the material (visual), recording and listening to a summary of what you have learned (auditory), and writing out the major points on index cards and arranging them into a logical sequence (kinesthetic). Personally, I recommend choosing three or four strategies from your preferred style, and a couple from each of the other two styles. Focus your efforts where your strengths lie, but always strive to incorporate multiple learning modalities (i.e. visual, auditory, and kinesthetic) into each study session.

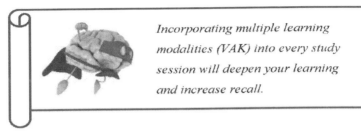

Incorporating multiple learning modalities (VAK) into every study session will deepen your learning and increase recall.

Multiple Intelligences

"Everyone is a genius. But if you judge a fish on its ability to climb a tree, it will live its whole life believing that it is stupid."
– Albert Einstein

In his ground-breaking book *Frames of Mind*, Harvard professor of education Howard Gardner describes his "Theory of Multiple Intelligences." This theory states that intelligence is not a fixed quantity that can be described by a single number, such as IQ. Intelligence is actually a set of skills that can be improved with use. Howard Gardner describes intelligence as "an ability to solve a problem or fashion a product that is valued in one or more cultural settings." In *Frames of Mind*, Dr. Gardner describes seven distinct intelligences. In 1996, he added an eighth intelligence (naturalistic intelligence) to the original list of seven. The eight intelligences are described below.

Linguistic/Verbal Intelligence: the ability to communicate using words. People with high linguistic intelligence speak fluently and write well. They usually learn well from books, like to write things down in their own words, have an excellent vocabulary, and are good at explaining things to others.

Logical/Mathematical Intelligence: the ability to calculate and think in a logical step-by-step manner. People with high logical intelligence are good with systems and numbers. They usually like to solve problems and puzzles, arrange tasks in a sensible order, and are good at recognizing patterns and relationships between things.

Visual/Spatial Intelligence: the ability to visualize and think in pictures. People with a high visual intelligence are good at imagining future results in their mind's eye. They usually enjoy learning from films and video, have a good sense of direction, and often see things that others don't notice.

Musical Intelligence: the ability to create and interpret music. People with a high musical intelligence have a good sense of rhythm and a deep appreciation for music. They often sing well, play a musical instrument, easily retain song lyrics, and enjoy musical performances, as well as natural sounds such as ocean waves.

Bodily/Kinesthetic Intelligence: the ability to present ideas and solve problems using bodily skills. People with a high bodily intelligence are coordinated and have excellent manual dexterity. They often play sports, do arts and crafts, enjoy hands-on learning, and take things apart to figure out how they work.

Interpersonal Intelligence: the ability to relate well and work effectively with others. People with a high interpersonal intelligence are sensitive to the moods of others and are good at reading people's emotions. They often make people feel comfortable and at ease, get involved in community activities and clubs, enjoy working with others, and are good at displaying empathy and understanding.

Intrapersonal Intelligence: the ability to understand and control one's own behavior and innermost feelings. People with a high interpersonal intelligence are independent and skilled at self analysis and reflection. They often appreciate quiet and privacy while working, set goals for their future, and can easily explain their decisions to others.

Naturalistic Intelligence: the ability to sense patterns in and make connections to the natural world. People with a high naturalistic intelligence have a strong sensitivity to nature and are good at categorizing plants and animals. They are usually keenly aware of their surroundings and enjoy spending time in the outdoors.

Most people tend to be stronger in some of the intelligences than in others. (You can do a Google search for "multiple intelligences test" to find online tests you can take to help determine your dominant intelligences.) One of the problems with our educational system is that most subjects are taught using only two intelligences: linguistic/verbal and logical/mathematical. If your strengths lie in one of the other six intelligences, then there is a good chance that you find formal classroom learning to be challenging.

The good news, however, is that no matter how the material is presented in class, you get to choose how to explore and play with the subject matter on your own time. Presented below are several different learning strategies you can use for each of the eight intelligences.

Linguistic/Verbal Intelligence

- Paraphrase the material – put it in your own words.
- Create a summary of all the important information and read aloud using different emotional tones (angry, happy, surprised, …).
- Write a newsletter or magazine article explaining the subject.

Logical/Mathematical Intelligence:

- List the main points in a logical numbered sequence.
- Create a flowchart or timeline.
- Question the validity of what you have just learned. Ask the following questions:

> *"Is this fact or opinion?"*
> *"What assumptions are being made?"*
> *"What is the evidence for this?"*
> *"What is another example or illustration of this?"*
> *"What conclusions can I draw from this information?"*

Visual/Spatial Intelligence:

- Create a learning map.
- Visualize the material in your mind's eye.
- Create a mental TV documentary on the material.
- Make a poster or video summarizing the subject.

Musical Intelligence:

- Write a song or jingle summarizing the material.
- Listen to classical music while studying.

Bodily/Kinesthetic Intelligence:

- Write notes on index cards, and sort them in a logical order.
- Make a model.
- Act out what you are learning.

Interpersonal Intelligence:

- Discuss what you have learned with someone.
- Find someone who knows more than you do, and ask them questions.
- Compare your notes with someone.
- Teach the material to a friend.

Intrapersonal Intelligence:

- Reflect on why the subject matters to you and how it fits in with what you already know.
- Read about the background of the people involved.
- Keep a journal in which you record your thoughts and reactions to what you are learning.

Naturalistic Intelligence:

Naturalistic intelligence is somewhat limited in its usefulness for exploring a subject. However, it is useful for providing an "ecological" check on the social and environmental implications of what you are learning. You can ask yourself the following questions:

- *"Are there any social or environmental implications to what I am learning? If so, what are they?"*
- *"Can this information be used to help solve any social or environmental issues?"*
- *"How might this information affect future generations?"*
- *"Can I use this information to better understand individuals and/or social behaviors?"*
- *"Does this information guide me to take any action?"*

Regardless of which of the eight intelligences is your strongest, you will learn more effectively if you involve multiple intelligences. Ideally, you would use all eight intelligences to explore the material you're learning. Although this may not be possible for all subjects, the more intelligences you can use, the better.

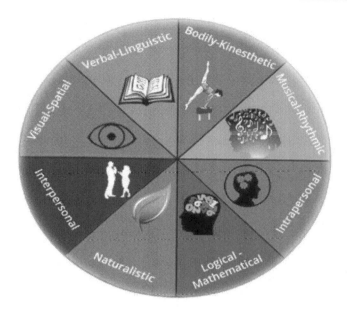

Experiment with the above techniques and strategies to see which ones work best for you. Everyone learns differently – only you can determine how you learn best. As you try out new techniques, be light, have fun, and stay curious. Learning how you learn best is a skill that takes practice and revision.

The most important way to use this information about learning styles and multiple intelligences is to develop your own personal "learning toolkit", which you draw upon to thoroughly explore and learn any subject. Just remember to always start with the big picture and incorporate different learning techniques and strategies every time you study. Keep at it … with the proper "learning toolkit", you'll be able to learn anything quickly and efficiently!

"No matter what the level of your ability, you have more potential than you can ever develop in a lifetime."

– James T. McCay

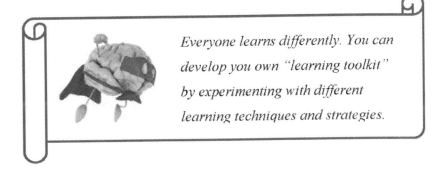

Everyone learns differently. You can develop you own "learning toolkit" by experimenting with different learning techniques and strategies.

Show You Know

1) Starting with the _____ _____ makes the learning process more efficient and increases recall.

2) What are the three primary learning styles?

3) According to Howard Gardner, intelligence is a fixed quantity that can be described by a single number such as IQ. True or False?

4) My primary learning style is _____. My dominant intelligence is _____.

Answers:

1) Big picture.
2) Visual, auditory, and kinesthetic (VAK).
3) False. Intelligence is a set of skills that can be improved with use.
4) Only you can answer these questions. Take the time to figure out the answers so you can develop your own personal "learning toolkit".

Step 3: Cement the Learning

After we have acquired the skills and knowledge, the next step in accelerated learning is to make sure the information gets stored into our long-term memory. After all, learning something new does us no good if we can't remember it. The good news is that your memory is already excellent. If you think yours isn't, take a moment to consider the countless number of words, facts, images, and other items that you have already memorized.

In reality, there is no such thing as a good memory or a bad memory, only a trained or untrained memory. In a fascinating book called *Moonwalking With Einstein*, journalist Joshua Foer decided to train for the US Memory Championship, after covering the World Memory Championship for a magazine article. Even though Joshua considered his memory to be poor, he won the US Memory Championship after training for only a year. His story is not unique. Anyone can improve their memory. All it takes is practice and proper technique. Listed below are eleven memory techniques and principles that you can use to improve your long-term memory.

1) Make a Decision to Remember

Many times, we forget new information simply because we never really registered it in the first place. How many times have you met someone for the first time and forgot their name within a few minutes or even seconds? How is that possible? The most likely reason is because you never really registered their name in the first place. Immediately after you take in new information such as somebody's name, make a conscious decision to remember it. The simple act of consciously deciding to remember something greatly enhances the probability of remembering it. The more determined you are, the more likely you will be to remember.

Speaking of remembering names, let me share with you an easy three step process (developed by Jim Kwik of <u>Kwik Learning</u>) that you can use the next time you meet someone new.

1) Pick a place on the person's face.
2) Imagine the name as a "sounds-like" image.
3) Entwine the two in a crazy picture that has action and exaggeration.

This process can be remembered with the acronym PIE (Pick a place, Imagine the name, Entwine the two).

Here is how you might use this technique. Let's say that at a friend's party you meet Shelly:

- **P**ick a place on Shelly's face. You decide to pick her nose (no pun intended).
- **I**magine her name as a "sounds-like" picture. For example, Shelly rhymes with deli so you picture a deli sandwich.
- **E**ntwine deli sandwich with Shelly's nose by picturing a steady stream of tiny deli sandwiches pouring uncontrollably from her nose.

Or, let's say you meet Joel at a local coffee shop:

- **P**ick a place: his eyes.
- **I**magine the name: a bowl of coal (which rhymes with Joel).
- **E**ntwine the two: picture two giant black bowls of coal where Joel's eyes should be.

This technique is even more effective if the facial feature that you choose stands out in some way, so you associate the feature with the person. In the previous examples, the entwined images (and hence the names) would be even more memorable if Shelly had a distinctive nose, and Joel had dark black eyes. This is because our memories are greatly enhanced when we create associations, which is the very topic of our next memory technique.

2) Association

Our memories work best through association. If you can associate something new with something you already know, you will be more likely to remember it. This is because we remember things that have meaning for us, and associations create meaning. Therefore, one of the keys to creating long-term memories is deliberately connecting new information to old information. The more associations we make, the better. Let's do a quick test. Please close your eyes and take 12 seconds to think of the color yellow, and things that are yellow. Ready, set, go ...

Did you think of things that are yellow? Good, then let me tell you about something called meaning networks. Let's say that some of the things that you thought of and associate with yellow were the sun, school buses, tennis balls, and lemons. If I could look inside your brain, I would find that the specific neurons that store your memories for the sun, school buses, tennis balls, and lemons are all physically connected together. This is a meaning network – a group of neurons that have a common association (things that are yellow), and are physically connected together.

As a student, when you associate new information with something you already know, you are physically connecting neurons together in a meaning network. As you make more associations, you also make more connections. This deepens the learning and makes it easier to recall the information from long-term memory.

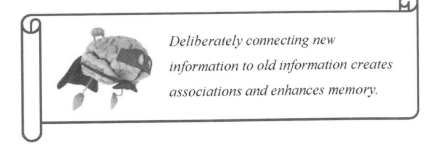

Deliberately connecting new information to old information creates associations and enhances memory.

3) Deliberately Create Multi-Sensory Memories

It has been said that on average, most people remember:

- 20% of what they read
- 30% of what they hear
- 40% of what they see
- 50% of what they say
- 60% of what they do
- 90% of what they see, hear, say, and do

While the above numbers are not scientifically accurate, the general trend is correct. The more senses you use when learning something new, the more likely you are to remember it. This is because our brain stores different kinds of memories (visual, auditory, and kinesthetic) in different parts of the brain.

The more locations within the brain where a particular memory is stored, the easier it is to recall that memory at a later time.

If you want to create strong, long-lasting memories, make a deliberate effort to involve as many of your senses as possible. Use learning techniques and strategies outlined in the previous chapter that combine reading, hearing, seeing, saying, and doing. Concentrate your efforts on where your natural abilities lie, but don't forget to involve as many of your senses as possible.

"Tell me and I forget, teach me and I may remember, involve me and I learn."

– Benjamin Franklin

The more senses you use while learning, the stronger the memory will be stored.

Memory Test Anyone?

Before we move on to the next two memory techniques, we need to pause for a little test. Don't worry and please don't get your amygdala all fired up! This is a simple memory test designed to illustrate the next two techniques we will learn. For this test, you will need the following: a stopwatch or timer, a piece of paper, and a pen. In fact, why don't you pause now and make sure that you have everything ready. I'll wait right here.

Welcome back. I missed you. ☺

On the next page is a list of 20 different words. After you turn the page, give yourself exactly 41 seconds to memorize as many of the 20 words as possible. When time is up, put the book down. Then, get the pen and paper and write down as many of the 20 words as you can in one minute. When you're finished, continue on to the next page to see how you did.

Memory Test

Remember, you have exactly 41 seconds to memorize as many of the 20 words listed below as you can. When time is up, write down as many of the 20 words as you can in one minute.

Ready, set, go!

Eraser	Pizza	Dahlia	Grace
Meadow	Pencil	Odor	Dandelion
Comfort	Beige	Cereal	Tree
Bacon	Chair	Bigfoot	Stream
Desk	Paper Clip	Juice	Sandwich

Remember!

So how did you do?

How many of the 20 words were you able to memorize in 41 seconds?

If you are like most people, you remembered roughly half of the 20 words. And, if you are like most people, the words that you remembered include eraser, cereal, and sandwich. So why those three words in particular? The answers will be revealed in the next two memory techniques.

4) Take Regular Breaks

The reason why most people remember eraser and sandwich has to do with the order in which something is learned. The order in which we learn information affects how reliably it will be recalled at a later time. This is known as the serial-position effect or the primacy-recency effect. This effect, which was first studied by Hermann Ebbinghaus in the 1880's, states that we tend to remember the most from the beginning (primacy) and the end (recency) of a study list. This is shown graphically below for the percentage of words recalled as a function of their position in a sequence.

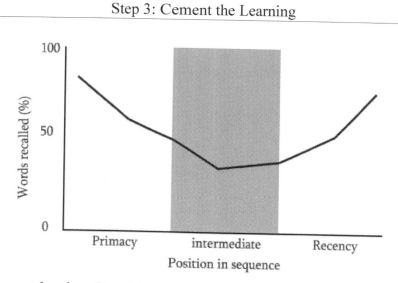

Image taken from http://en.wikipedia.org/wiki/Serial_position_effect

   The primacy-recency effect doesn't only apply to remembering a list of words. It also applies to material presented during class or learned during a study session. In essence, we tend to remember the most at the beginning and the end of a learning session. This means that if we want to maximize our learning and keep recall high, it makes sense to have a lot of beginnings and endings. How can we do this? It's quite simple really. We can increase the number of beginnings and endings by taking frequent breaks.

   Whenever studying, it is much better to break a long study session up into several mini-sessions, with breaks in between. In general, I recommend that you take a break about every 45 minutes. The break should be about 5 to 10 minutes long, and it should be a complete rest from what you were doing. Don't take a break from one subject to work on another. Get up and move your body in some way. I recommend spending a few minutes stretching, and then recharging with water and a light snack, if necessary.

This is really a great bit of knowledge to have as a student. Think about it. You can actually remember more by taking more breaks. Learn more and study less. That's what accelerated learning is all about!

5) Make the Information Stand Out

I bet that you already know why cereal is one of the words that most people remember. It's because the word cereal stands out from all the other words – it is bold and boxed.

The ability to find and take notice of things that stand out from everything else was an important survival skill back in prehistoric times. Hence, our brains have evolved to become very good at noticing differences. Information that stands out in some way grabs our attention and redirects our focus. That information could be the presence of a saber-toothed tiger or a vocabulary term you need to memorize for a quiz. Whatever it is, the more the information stands out from everything else, the more memorable it will be – and the more likely it will get stored in your long-term memory.

An easy way to take advantage of this fact, as a student, is to add color and pictures to your notes. Make important information from your notes stand out in some way. I recommend that you go beyond using just a highlighter. Use multiple colors, and add small icons or pictures. A lot of my students use the Bic pens with the four different colors (black, blue, green, and red) that you can click. Whenever I change colored markers on the white board, I am greeted by a symphony of clicks from my students. ☺

You can also add color and images to your notes after class. A really, really great practice (I mean it – really, really great) that you can adopt, as a student, is to review your notes after class. The sooner after the class, the better – definitely before the next class meeting. As you review your notes, first make sure that you understand everything you wrote, and that you fill in any possible gaps. Then use different colors to highlight important information in some way. Be creative … develop your own color code and style. Have fun and add personal touches. It's an easy and enjoyable way to make your notes more memorable as you refire neural connections.

We tend to remember information that stands out from the rest. Adding color and images to your notes can make them more memorable.

6) Organize the Information Meaningfully

We remember information better when it is organized than when it is disorganized. If you want to learn something and remember it, take the time to paraphrase the information in your own words. Organize it into categories that are meaningful to you. This process of paraphrasing and organizing requires that you really think about and understand the material, and will greatly enhance your level of recall. Another reason that organizing the information into meaningful categories enhances memory is because it also creates associations. And, as I am sure you remember, the more associations you make, the stronger the memory is stored.

Meaningful organization is especially useful if you have to memorize a list of words, such as a shopping list. For example, let's say you had to memorize the list of 20 words from the memory test, and you had more time. You could organize the information into the following categories:

Office items: Eraser, Desk, Pencil, Chair, Paper clip
Food: Bacon, Pizza, Cereal, Juice, Sandwich
Outdoors: Meadow, Dahlia, Dandelion, Tree, Stream, Bigfoot
Other: Comfort, Beige, Odor, Grace

Remembering the categories will help you remember the items in the category. Here is a great bonus tip at no extra charge:

A fun way to remember all of the items from one category is to tie them together into a crazy mental image or movie. For example, to remember all of the food words, you could imagine spilling a tall glass of *bacon juice* (doh!) into your *cereal* so you have to eat *pizza sandwiches* for breakfast. Or to remember the outdoor words, you could imagine *Bigfoot* swinging from a *tree* next to a *stream* in a beautiful *meadow*. Behind each ear, Bigfoot has a giant flower: a giant *dandelion* and a giant *dahlia*.

One last note about remembering words from the memory test before we move on. Two of the words from the list that are least well remembered are comfort and grace. The reason is because comfort and grace are abstract concepts, and are hard to visualize. In general, we remember the concrete better than the abstract. Visual memory is our strongest. If we can't form a clear image of something in our mind's eye, it is very difficult for us to remember it.

7) Create a Mnemonic

A mnemonic is simply a memory device that is used to remember larger pieces of information. There are many types of mnemonics. The most common type is a word mnemonic, in which the first letter of each item in a list is arranged to form a word or phrase. For example, many people remember the colors of the spectrum (Red, Orange, Yellow, Green, Blue, Indigo, Violet) using the mnemonic ROY G BIV. Another example is "Please Excuse My Dear Aunt Sally", which is used to remember the order of operations: Parentheses, Exponents, Multiply, Divide, Add, and Subtract.

I have used several word mnemonics, or acronyms, in this book to help you remember different concepts. Do you remember what the acronyms PACER, FAST, VAK, and PIE stand for? I hope so. If not, here is a quick reminder:

PACER: (Prepare your state, Acquire the skills and knowledge, Cement the learning, Examine and embrace, Review, revise, and reward)

FAST: (Fear, Anxiety, Stress, and Threat)

VAK: (Visual, Auditory, Kinesthetic)

PIE: (Pick a place, Imagine the name, and Entwine the two)

Another common type of mnemonic is a rhyme mnemonic, in which information is put into the form of a poem or song that rhymes. For example, "I before E, except after C, or when sounding like A, as in neighbor or weigh."

A very powerful mnemonic, and an easy way to remember numbers, is to make a sentence with the number of letters in each word representing a number. For example, you can remember the first 15 digits of pi, which are 3.14159265358979, by using the following sentence: "Boy I need a drink, alcoholic of course, after the heavy lectures involving quantum mechanics." (Boy = 3, I = 1, need = 4, a = 1, drink = 5, ..., quantum = 7, mechanics = 9) This can be very useful for remembering phone numbers, PINs, and important dates. For example, the PIN for my Wells Fargo bank card is 4235, which I remember with "Show me the money". (Mental note to self: be sure to change my PIN before I publish.)

When remembering years, it is customary to drop off the 1 from the year and use 10 letters for the number zero. For example, here are a few dates of personal significance and how I remember them:

- 1542: (the year that Juan Cabrillo explored the California coast): Coast Juan CA
- 1906: (the year of the great San Francisco earthquake): Francisco earthquake struck
- 1945: (the year the first atomic bomb was built as part of the Manhattan Project): Manhattan make bombs
- 1955: (the year Einstein died): Einstein's final hours

Notice that the words I use are related to the actual date in some way. This is important because you need to remember the sentence or phrase you created, in order to remember the date.

You will find that the more you use this technique of letting the numbers of letters in each word represent a number, the easier it will become. You also can use this technique for things like your checking account number, your credit card number, your license plate, your friends' birthdays … if you are having any trouble with this, email me your credit card number, and I will help you create a memorable sentence that you can use. ☺

8) Set it to Music

Music is an extremely useful learning tool. In fact, it is much more powerful than most people think. In addition to integrating the left and right sides of our brains, it also stimulates the emotional control center (the amygdala) of our brain. Because emotions are strongly linked to long-term memory, music is a **very** powerful memory tool! Think about how many songs you know by heart. For me, it is hundreds. Did you *consciously* try to learn the lyrics to all of them? My guess is that less than half of the songs you know by heart were through conscious effort on your part. Personally, I still know the lyrics to songs that my mom used to play on the record player more than 30 years ago.

A great way to use music as a study tool/memory aid is to take a well known song, jingle, or TV advertisement, and write your own words to the familiar melody. Replace the lyrics of the familiar song with the information that you want to remember. The process of writing your own words serves as a valuable review and requires that you think about and understand the material. After you have the song written, sing it out loud multiple times, with the melody playing in the background. (If you chose a popular song, you can find a karaoke version of the song to use.) Continue to sing your new song until you have it memorized. Then, periodically review your song over the next few days, to ensure that it gets stored into long-term memory.

This technique of writing your own "educational songs" is extremely effective. There is just something about music that makes it stick in our memory. Do you think that you could ever forget your ABCs? This technique is also quite fun once you get into it. Give it a try, and I think you will agree.

While we are on the subject of music, there are many students I know who think that they study better when listening to the kind of music that they normally enjoy (electronic, rock, contemporary, indie …). The fact is that they don't. When we listen to music that has lyrics, some of our valuable brain space is used processing the words to the song. Our working memory can only focus on one thing at a time. Multitasking does not exist. What happens is that our focus rapidly jumps from one thing to another, and then back again. If you listen to music with lyrics while studying, your focus will constantly jump back and forth between what you are studying and what you are listening to. This will decrease your overall comprehension and recall of the material.

Multitasking does not exist. Listening to music with lyrics while studying splits our attention and decreases recall.

However, as we learned previously, Baroque music can have a positive impact on learning. Recall that Baroque music is a specific genre of classical music with a steady 50 to 80 beats per minute that was composed between ~1600 and 1750. Playing Baroque music can help promote the relaxed yet alert mental state (the alpha brain-wave state) that is optimal for learning. When playing Baroque music while studying, make sure to keep the volume low. You want the music to be background noise, so that it is barely audible.

9) Memory Flashing

Memory flashing is a very simple, yet very effective memory technique. It's great for memorizing information that can be presented visually, such as in a list, a mind map, or some other kind of visual representation. Personally, I use memory flashing to learn all of my students' names the first week of classes. Here's how. First, I create a Microsoft Word document with all of my students' individual pictures placed into tables. Next, I print out a master copy and write all of their names next to their pictures. I study their names and faces for around five minutes and put away the master copy. I then print out another copy with just pictures, and try to remember all of their names. I say their names out loud as I go through the pictures. I also rewrite their names on the new copy. Next, I compare the new copy with the master copy, taking note of any names I got wrong. Then, I study the master copy again for a few minutes before trying to remember all of their names again. I repeat this process of studying, testing, and comparing again and again until I feel confident I have all of my student's names memorized. This usually takes me about a half hour for a class of 50 students. Over the next few days, I periodically review the master copy to cement the learning.

The above example of learning student's names is what memory flashing is all about: study, test, compare, and then repeat. To begin memory flashing, you make notes by creating a mind map, or brief list of important points. For example's sake, let's say that you are memorizing a list of important points for an essay question. First, study the list for a few minutes, then put it away. Then, test yourself by trying to re-create the list from memory. After you are finished, compare your new list to the original. Your brain will quickly notice anything that you missed. Study the original again, and then make a third list from memory - again compare with the original. Continue this process until the two lists are the same. When recreating the list, I recommend you say the list out loud and rewrite it each time. It will involve more senses and increase recall. As a final note, to make sure that you cement the list into long-term memory, it is important to get a good night's sleep and then periodically review the list over the next few days. As luck would have it, those are the subjects of our next two memory techniques.

10) Sleep on it

As a student, it is not uncommon to sacrifice sleep in order to study or engage in social activities. I know that I did. We are all busy, and it sometimes feels as if we have no other choice. However, simply put, sacrificing sleep is a very bad idea. Lack of sleep negatively affects almost every aspect of learning that is important for academic success. As stated by Dr. John Medina in *Brain Rules*: *"The bottom line is that sleep loss means mind loss. Sleep loss cripples thinking, in just about every way you can measure thinking. Sleep loss hurts attention, executive function, working memory, mood, quantitative skills, logical reasoning ability, and general math knowledge."*

Please take a moment and reread the above quote. Did you read it again? Good, because it is a great summary of just how important getting a good night's sleep is to learning. Sleep loss cripples thinking! That is why, as a student, getting adequate sleep is essential to your success. You just don't function well without it. A good night's sleep is especially important the night before an exam. Trying to think intensely under the pressures of an exam, without adequate sleep, is setting yourself up for disappointment. You are much better off going to bed at a reasonable hour than cramming until the wee hours of the morning.

Sleep loss also cripples long-term memory. Recent research has shown that long-term memories are stored in our brains while we are in theta state. This occurs during sleep, or when we are deeply relaxed. While we sleep, our brains are processing and storing the information we learned during our waking hours. Because of this, it is extremely important to get a good night's sleep if you want to retain what you have learned. An excellent study pattern to adopt is to learn the material in a variety of ways (as we covered earlier), briefly review the information before you go to bed, get a good night's sleep, and then briefly review the information again in the morning.

Sleep loss cripples thinking and long-term memory. A good night's sleep is crucial to your success.

11) Review the Material Frequently

As a popular saying goes, "repetition is the mother of learning." This is true for pretty much anything that we want to learn. The more we review, the better we remember. If we want to really learn something and commit it to long-term memory, we must have repeated exposure over time, so our neural connections become well established.

Whenever we learn something new, we are basically connecting neurons together in new ways, creating a new path through our dense forest of neurons. And just like an animal path in the forest, the more times that path is used, the more established it becomes. This is especially true for the neural connections that we make when we learn something new. We need to use that path, and refire those same neurons, by reviewing the information at frequent intervals.

So how often should you review the information? There is no definitive answer to that question. Well, yes there is. The more often, the better. Ideally, you would review and study a little bit every day. How long depends on what and how much you are reviewing. Every day may not be possible, but the more consistent you are, the better. If you are a student, I recommend that you get into the habit of working on each subject a little bit at least five days a week. Remember, the more you use the path, the more established it will become. Plus, the return on your time is huge.

I generally think of frequent review sessions as yielding approximately a 50% return on my time. This means that I get the same (if not more) benefit from studying two hours spread out over a few days (say 30 minutes a night for four nights), than from studying three hours in a single night. Accelerated learning is all about efficiency. Frequent review sessions are one of the keys to learning and remembering more in less time.

As a final note, information stored in our memory won't stay there forever if we don't use it. We still need to review the information periodically if we want to remember it long term. As you have probably experienced as a student, if you don't use material from a class, it starts to fade from your memory. Have you ever forgotten how to do something that you learned just the previous semester? I know that if I haven't taught a class in a few semesters, I still have to review my notes to remind myself of certain equations. That's just how our brains work – use it or lose it.

Here is a great strategy you can use to help prevent memory fade. Once a month, schedule an hour or two that is solely dedicated to reviewing old material. If you're currently taking classes, you can review each class from the beginning to where you are now. You can also review notebooks from previous classes - anything that you want to "keep fresh" and commit to long-term memory. Keep in mind that the goal is not to learn new information, but to cement the knowledge you already have. I recommend a 45-minute review session, followed by a 10-minute break, and then another 45-minute review session. If possible, schedule the review for the same date each month, and be consistent. Give it a try. You'll be amazed at the tremendous benefit you get from the small but consistent investment of your time.

So there you have it – eleven memory techniques and principles. These techniques will improve your long-term memory, and become important allies on your journey toward academic mastery. The more you use these techniques, the faster your memory will improve. However, please be patient. Powerful memory requires practice. Continue using these techniques, and they will eventually become second nature.

"Memory is the treasury and guardian of all things."
– Cicero

Show You Know

1) You are either born with a good memory or a bad memory. True or False?

2) The more _____ you use while learning, the stronger the memory will be stored.

3) What is the recency-primacy effect?

4) Which of the following was not one of the 11 memory techniques and principles discussed in this chapter?

   a) Association.
   b) Make the information stand out.
   c) Set it to music.
   d) Review the material frequently.

Answers:

1) False. Anyone can improve their memory with practice and proper technique.
2) Senses.
3) The recency-primacy effect (also known as the serial-position effect) states that we tend to remember the most at the beginning and end of any learning session.
4) This is a trick question. They were all discussed in this chapter. ☺

Step 4: Examine and Embrace

"The unexamined life is not worth living."

– Socrates

Congratulations – we've made it through the bulk of accelerated learning techniques. The first three steps contained **a lot** of information. It's all downhill from here. The last two steps are quick, easy to learn, and fun to apply. Before we continue the rest of our journey together, let's pause for a quick one paragraph summary of the first three steps.

In the first step of accelerated learning, we prepare our state for learning. Spending just a few minutes preparing our mental, emotional, and physical states can literally double our learning. After we've gotten into the optimal state, the second step is acquiring the skills and knowledge. First, we spend time getting the "big picture", so our brain has an overview of how everything fits together. Then, we acquire the information using a variety of techniques that incorporate different learning styles and intelligences. After that, the third step of accelerated learning is cementing the knowledge into long-term memory. We do that by using a set of simple techniques and strategies to improve our recall of what we've just learned.

Congratulations again! We refired neural connections and further established the new paths we've recently created. Let's continue our journey.

The fourth step of the accelerated learning process is to "examine and embrace" our newly acquired skills and knowledge. We do this by first examining our knowledge and testing ourselves using different learning techniques that we already know. Our goal is to show ourselves (and others) that we understand and remember the information. Then, we embrace the knowledge by practicing what we've just learned. Remember, our brains work under the principle of use it or lose it. If we want to retain our new skills and knowledge long term, we must put them into practice. The more we practice, the more confident and fluent we become, further cementing our knowledge into long-term memory.

Examine Your Knowledge

In the first part of step four, we examine our knowledge and test our understanding of what we've just learned. This is really just a straightforward check of our ability using any of the previously discussed strategies that worked well for us. Hopefully, you've had a chance to experiment with some of the different learning techniques and strategies and develop you own learning toolkit. If not, there is no better time to start than the present. Either way, you will no doubt find that some strategies and techniques work better for you than others. These are the ones that you want to use when testing yourself. Some possibilities may include:

- Testing yourself with flash cards.
- Explaining what you've learned to someone else.
- Recreating your notes from memory.
- Reconstructing a learning map or list of important points.
- Reviewing the material out loud to yourself.
- Partnering with a study buddy and quizzing each other.
- Creating a mental movie of what you've learned.
- Taking online quizzes and exams from trusted internet sources.

As you examine your knowledge and test yourself, there are two important points to consider:

First, be sure to incorporate what you already know from the first three steps of accelerated learning. For example, here are some strategies you might use the next time you sit down to review and test yourself:

- Reflect on WHY learning this material is important.
- Get into alpha state before reviewing.
- Listen to Baroque music at low volume while reviewing.
- Set a specific learning goal for the review session.
- Make sure you have the big picture of how everything fits together.
- Use study techniques that incorporate different learning modalities (VAK).

- Use study techniques that incorporate multiple intelligences.
- Review in 45-minute chunks followed by a 10-minute break.
- Use different memory techniques to cement the learning.

Second, be sure to have fun while reviewing. The more fun you have, the better. Recall that positive emotions are vital to the learning process. Our brains function most efficiently when we are happy, and least efficiently when we are stressed or anxious. I'm not saying that examining your knowledge should be a party, but do what you can to make the process as enjoyable as possible. You will learn faster and retain more of what you've learned.

"People rarely succeed unless they have fun in what they are doing."

– Dale Carnegie

When you examine your knowledge, make sure to have fun and incorporate accelerated learning techniques.

A quick side note for current students: you will usually get a chance to examine your knowledge when you take a quiz or exam on the material you've been learning. However, I strongly recommend testing yourself before that happens. A great habit to develop as a student is to become your own judge of how well you know the material. Don't wait for the quiz or exam. Use your favorite learning techniques to test yourself before you are tested formally. Just make sure to allow yourself enough time to correct any possible gaps in your knowledge. This means not waiting until the night before a quiz or exam to test yourself.

Being your own judge of how well you know the material applies to class assignments as well. Develop the habit of checking your own work for completeness and quality control. Mentally grade all of your work before you turn it in. This applies to anything you will receive a grade on, such as problem sets, lab reports, essay questions, short-answer questions, papers, or take-home exams. When you get your graded work back, compare the grade you received with the grade you gave yourself. Then make a plan for how you will improve next time. Your goal should be to show incremental improvements on each new assignment, until you are getting and maintaining the grades you want.

Embrace Your Knowledge

After we have examined and tested our understanding of the material, the next step is to embrace the knowledge and put it into practice. You can't learn to ride a bike by simply reading a book. You have to go out and ride the bike, fall down, pick yourself back up, and then try again. The same thing is true for learning any new skill or subject. You must practice the skill and put it to use in order to master it.

Do you remember how difficult driving was the first few times you tried it? I do and it seemed like there were a thousand different things I had to think about. Now, driving is second nature for me, as I'm sure it is for most of you. Why? Because we have practiced driving so many times that it has become habituated behavior. The neural pathways associated with driving are so well established that we hardly have to think about it anymore.

This is what we want to happen with any new skill or knowledge that we learn. We want the neural pathways to become so well established that the skill becomes second nature, just like driving. The only way for that to happen is through repeated practice. The accelerated learning techniques presented in this book will help you streamline the process and make it more efficient. However, there is no way around the requirement of having to practice and embrace a new skill in order to master it.

Many of us think that smart, talented, and successful people were just born that way. This couldn't be farther from the truth. People who are experts in their field are experts because they have practiced until the skill/knowledge has become automatic. People like to think that superstars like Michael Jordan are great because of some natural inborn talent. What they don't think about are the thousands of hours of practice it took Jordan to become a superstar, or the many mistakes he made along the way. (Note: Michael Jordan was actually cut from his high school varsity basketball team as a sophomore. This motivated him to spend countless hours practicing on the court.)

"I've missed more than 9000 shots in my career. I've lost almost 300 games. 26 times, I've been trusted to take the game winning shot and missed. I've failed over and over and over again in my life. And that is why I succeed."

– Michael Jordan

Speaking of mistakes, they are going to happen so be kind to yourself. You are learning a new skill, and it takes time to become proficient. As Albert Einstein said, *"Anyone who has never made a mistake has never tried anything new."* Mistakes are not only alright, they are, in fact, vital to the learning process. Mistakes provide us with valuable feedback and clarify areas that we need to explore more thoroughly.

"An expert is a person who has made all the mistakes that can be made in a very narrow field."

– Niels Bohr

As a final note, let me share with you an important distinction about practice. You have probably heard the expression "practice makes perfect". Well, this expression is wrong. Practice doesn't make perfect, practice makes permanent. It is only perfect practice that makes perfect. If we practice the wrong technique over and over again, we will eventually become very proficient at it. Therefore, you need to be very careful what you practice because you might get good at it.

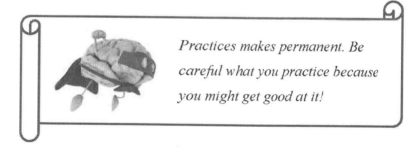

Practices makes permanent. Be careful what you practice because you might get good at it!

This concept applies to all areas of life. For example, if you regularly procrastinate, putting things off until the last minute, then that is what you will become good at. Similarly, if you are regularly late to meetings and social engagements, then you will become good at being late. As a student, it is extremely important that you are very conscious of both **what** and **how** you practice. The habits you develop as a student may stay with you for a very long time.

So, that's the fourth step of accelerated learning. Examine your knowledge to test your understanding of the material, and then embrace the knowledge so the neural pathways become well established. I told you it was quick and easy to learn. I like to think of the fourth step as applying cement to the pathways we've created during the first three steps.

Show You Know

1) What is the fourth step of accelerated learning?

2) Which strategies and techniques do we want to use when examining our knowledge?

3) _____ provide us with valuable feedback and clarify the areas we need to explore more thoroughly.

4) Practice makes perfect. True or False?

Answers:

1) Examine and Embrace.
2) The strategies and techniques that we've found work best for us.
3) Mistakes.
4) False. Practice makes permanent. Perfect practice makes perfect.

Step 5: Review, Revise, and Reward

"Celebrate what you want to see more of."

– Tom Peters

Well, here we are at the fifth and final step of accelerated learning. This last step, for all practical purposes, is really just a quick review of how the learning process went – followed by a celebration. Our goal is to revise the learning process, so we improve it the next time around. Then we reward ourselves, so we anchor positive emotions to learning.

Review and Revise

As we saw earlier, there are specific techniques and strategies that tend to work better for visual learners than for auditory or kinesthetic learners. The same is true for intelligences. Certain techniques and strategies tend to work better for someone whose dominant intelligence is logical/mathematical, than for someone whose dominant intelligence is linguistic/verbal. However, the key phrase here is "tend to". No two people learn in exactly the same way. Your personal learning style is as unique as your fingerprint. The only way to determine your learning style is through trial and error. You have to experiment with different techniques and see how they work for you. Learning how you learn best is a continual process of reflection and revision. It will not happen overnight but the effort is well worth it. Evaluating your own learning process is one of the keys to becoming a successful learner.

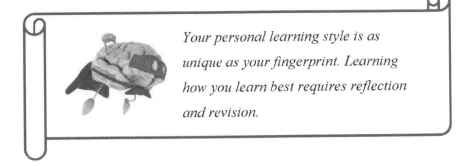

Your personal learning style is as unique as your fingerprint. Learning how you learn best requires reflection and revision.

Some guiding questions that you can ask yourself include:

- *"What went well?"*
- *"What didn't go well or could have gone better?"*
- *"How can I improve the learning process next time?"*
- *"If I was to learn this material again, what would I do differently?"*
- *"Which learning strategies did I enjoy the most?"*
- *"What learning strategies did I enjoy the least?"*
- *"Which learning strategies were the most useful for me?"*
- *"Which learning strategies were the least useful?"*
- *"Was I happy with my overall performance? If not, why?"*
- *"Did I use accelerated learning techniques to learn more efficiently?"*

You can ask these questions after a major assignment, after a quiz or exam, at the end of the academic quarter/semester, or at the end of the school year. As you first start using accelerated learning techniques, I recommend asking yourself these questions frequently, at least once every few weeks, if not more often. If you are taking multiple classes, it is useful to ask these questions for each and every class. You might find that certain strategies work well for you in one subject but not another.

It's beneficial to keep track of the answers to these questions in a learning journal/log. You can use the journal to track your improvement as you continue to tackle new learning projects. This gives a sense of progress, which is critical for both motivation and success.

"Without continual growth and progress, such words as improvement, achievement, and success have no meaning."
– Benjamin Franklin

Reward

The very last step of accelerated learning is to celebrate and reward our success. This step is so important and yet so often overlooked. The purpose of rewarding our success is twofold. First, it gives us a sense of completion and marks the end of a job well done. The reward is something that we can look forward to, especially when the going gets tough. Second, it helps our brains link positive emotions to learning. We want learning to be enjoyable so we continue to do it throughout our entire lives. The more fun we associate with learning, the more likely we will be to continue doing it.

The reward we give ourselves does not have to be an extravagant affair or cost a lot of money. In fact, many of the best rewards cost very little or nothing at all. Listed below are 25 ideas for inexpensive rewards to help you celebrate your success:

- Take a long deep breath and reflect on your success.
- Share your accomplishment with friends and family. This can be done in person, over the phone, or by text or email.
- Share your success on Twitter or Facebook.
- Write your success down, and post it where you can see it every day.
- Take a nap or give yourself permission to sleep in the next day.
- Thank everyone who helped you accomplish your goal.
- Give someone a high five.
- Go outdoors and enjoy nature.
- Watch a movie or your favorite television show.
- Read a good book.
- Take a complete break from what you were doing and "veg out" for a while.
- Go for a walk (take your dog if you have one).

- Go to the gym and exercise.
- Put on upbeat music and have a quick 10-minute dance party.
- Keep a success journal.
- Visit with a good friend.
- Do an activity that you enjoy but rarely have time to do.
- Pay it forward and help someone else achieve their goal.
- Make your favorite dessert.
- Make an award for yourself, and hang it where you can see it.
- Attend a local art show or museum.
- Download a new song or app.
- Take a 30-minute break and play a game.
- Engage in one of your hobbies.
- Do something nice for someone else.

In order to get the most out of your reward and anchor positivity to learning, it is important that you celebrate immediately after your accomplishment. Do not wait, and do not start a new task without rewarding your effort. Otherwise, there is a good chance you will forget about the reward, especially if you're not already in the habit of celebrating your successes.

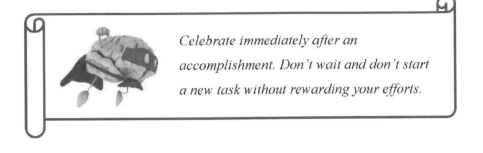

Celebrate immediately after an accomplishment. Don't wait and don't start a new task without rewarding your efforts.

"The more you praise and celebrate your life, the more there is in life to celebrate."

– Oprah Winfrey

You do not have to wait until you have completed a learning goal or project to reward yourself. I recommend that you develop the habit of scheduling rewards for studying between quizzes, exams, and major assignments. It can sometimes be difficult to remain motivated during those times when there are no upcoming deadlines, such as assignments or exams. Scheduling periodic rewards can help maintain your motivation and keep you moving forward on the path to success.

Show You Know

1) Learning how you learn best takes reflection and revision. True or False?

2) How often should you review and revise your learning process?

3) Rewarding our efforts helps to link _____ _____ to learning.

4) It doesn't matter when we reward ourselves as long as we celebrate our success. True or False?

Answers:

1) True.
2) At least every few weeks if not more often.
3) Positive emotions.
4) False. We want to reward ourselves immediately, before we move on to the next task.

Call to Action

"Experience has taught me that there is one chief reason why some people succeed and others fail. The difference is not one of knowing, but of doing. The successful man is not so superior in ability as in action. So far as success can be reduced to a formula, it consists of this: doing what you know you should do."

– Roger Babson

Regardless of what you want to be, do, or have, one of the keys to accomplishing any goal is learning what you need to learn. The techniques presented in this book will help you do that efficiently and effectively. The other key is taking action and doing what you need to do. That part is up to you.

Here is a quick riddle for you:

Three birds are sitting on a power line when one of the birds decides to fly away. How many birds are left?

And the answer is …

There are three birds left.

There is a big difference between deciding to do something and actually doing it. Don't decide that you are going to use the techniques presented in this book – go out and use them! Accelerated learning techniques are only useful if you apply them. I, therefore, challenge you to set a learning goal for yourself **right now**. If you are a student, choose your most difficult subject and apply these techniques. If you are working, choose to learn something that will help you excel in your present occupation. (The sad fact is that many people slave away at their jobs year after year, never taking the time to excel at what they do. Don't be one of those people.) You can also choose to learn a subject that you've always wanted to learn but thought was too difficult.

Whatever it is that you choose to learn, take action today. Don't be like the average person and procrastinate in applying these amazing techniques. After all, if you want to have above-average results, you have to be willing to do what the average person isn't willing to do. Establish a learning project today and demonstrate to yourself that you have the ability to learn/master any subject. You will be amazed at just how brilliant you really are.

Good luck and happy learning!

"Successful people aren't born that way. They become successful by establishing the habit of doing things that unsuccessful people don't like to do. The successful people don't always like these things themselves; they just get on and do them."

– Steve Ibbotson

Show You Know

1) What learning goal are you committed to achieving?

2) When will you achieve it?

3) Who can help support you with your goal?

4) Why is achieving this goal important to you?

Answers:
1) Write down your answer, and post it somewhere you'll see it every day.
2) Write the date down next to your goal.
3) Contact at least one of them within one week.
4) Make sure that you know your WHY.

Part 2:
But Wait, There's More!
Six Super Success
Strategies

Introduction

Although you now know the five steps of accelerated learning and how to apply them, our journey together is not over yet. I have more to share with you. Specifically, I want to share with you six super success strategies to help you get the most out of what you have already learned. These are strategies that will help you succeed in school, and in life.

Since we know that giving our brain the big picture is an important part of accelerated learning, here is a list of the six super success strategies we will soon be learning:

- Strategy #1: Take Effective Notes (Five Ninja Note-Taking Techniques)
- Strategy #2: Read Faster (Five Simple Steps to Double Your Reading Speed)
- Strategy #3: Set SMART Goals (Five Easy Strategies for Achieving SMART Goals)
- Strategy #4: Manage Your Time (Ten Time-Management Tips for the Busy Student)
- Strategy #5: Eat Healthy (Ten Brain-Healthy Foods for Smarter Eating)
- Strategy #6: Be Happy (Ten Proven Ways to Increase Happiness)

I decided to write these chapters in list format for quick reference and easy reading. The topics were chosen because I believe them all to be important ingredients for success, especially academic success. These are also topics that interest me personally, topics I want to stay current on, as I periodically update and revise this book. They didn't quite fit into the flow of the chapters on the five steps of accelerated learning, so I decided to include them as a separate section. Together with the five steps of accelerated learning, these six super success strategies will help you learn more in less time.

Strategy #1: Take Effective Notes (Five Ninja Note-Taking Techniques)

"Attending lectures without taking notes is like keeping your mouth open and hoping for a roast duck to fly in."

– R. Hummel

Let's start with a basic premise. Everyone should take notes during class (unless, of course, you have a learning disability that requires a note taker). As a teacher, I try not to use the word "should" too often; I don't want to "should" all over my students. However, it definitely applies in this case. Your notes are perhaps your single greatest tool for success in any class. Taking quality notes during class accomplishes three major goals that are vital for accelerated learning:

1) Taking notes adds a kinesthetic component to the learning process. You will already be taking in both auditory information through what the instructor says and visual information through what you see. Taking notes adds the kinesthetic component to round out the three learning styles (VAK).

2) Taking notes keeps you actively involved during class. Learning is not a spectator sport. You have to be involved and focused in order to learn; during class, that means taking notes. And not just any notes, but high-

quality notes using the techniques you will soon be learning.

3) Your class notes serve as a valuable reference for everything that you are learning. They will be one of your most effective resources for studying/reviewing the material. The more complete and detailed your notes are, the more benefit you will gain from them.

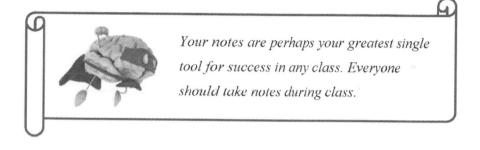

Your notes are perhaps your greatest single tool for success in any class. Everyone should take notes during class.

Before we jump into the five techniques, let me be clear that I am not presenting a new note-taking system for you to learn. There are many systems out there, such as <u>mind mapping</u> or the <u>Cornell Note-Taking System</u>, both of which are great by the way. I wanted to give you five easy techniques that you can use in any class - techniques that don't require learning an entirely new way of taking notes. These five ninja note-taking techniques can all be implemented immediately, starting with your very next class (hint, hint).

1) Preview the material before class.

The first note-taking technique begins before we even enter the classroom. It is previewing the material before class. I've mentioned this accelerated learning technique previously in terms of giving our brain the big picture of what we will be learning. Previewing the material is also a great technique for note taking.

It is difficult to take effective notes during class when we're exposed to the information for the very first time. Our brain's valuable resources are busy translating new vocabulary terms, deciphering what the instructor is saying, and making sense of how everything fits together. Taking effective notes while all of this is happening can be very challenging. Spending 10 to 15 minutes previewing the material before class introduces our brain to the vocabulary, concepts, and ideas we will be learning. This frees up our brain's valuable resources so we can better concentrate on taking effective notes.

Before we learn the next technique, let's pause for a brief experiment. Please close your eyes and think of a banana for seven seconds. Did you think of one? Good, then let me ask you two quick questions. First, did you think of an image of a banana or the word banana? Second, if you saw an image of a banana, was it in color or black and white?

If you are like most people, you pictured an image of a banana which was in color, most likely yellow. The reason you pictured a yellow banana is because this is how we tend to think, in color and in pictures. Unfortunately, this is not how many students tend to take notes.

2) Use images and color.

As we learned from our little banana experiment, we tend to think in pictures and in color. This is the exact opposite of how many students take notes. They use pencil only, and fill the pages of their notebook with words and equations. While there is nothing wrong with words and equations, if this is the only thing in your notebook, your brain isn't going to be very motivated to use your notes.

Adding color and images to your notes is an easy and fun way to make them more "brain-friendly". I recommend using three or four different colors, maybe five. Two colors are not enough, and more than five can be distracting. The images you add do not have to be detailed works of art. They can be question marks, stars, word balloons, stick figures, diagrams, smiley faces, icons, graphs, doodles, or anything else that you want. The goal of using color and pictures is to add flair to your notes, making them more visually appealing and memorable. (Note: For fans of the movie Office Space, the minimum number is 15 pieces of flair. ☺) You can add color and images during class if there is time. If not, you can always add them after class, when you actively review your notes (see #5 below).

3) Go beyond simply copying what the instructor writes.

Some instructors write class notes on a blackboard or whiteboard, some use PowerPoint slides, and some use transparencies. Regardless of how your teacher lectures, effective note taking means going beyond simply copying what they write on the board or show on an overhead. I know from experience that instructors present material that we don't always write down. If you only copy what the instructor writes, you will miss a lot of valuable information.

An important aspect of effective note taking is actively listening to the instructor and taking notes on what they say, in addition to what they write. This doesn't mean trying to copy down everything that comes out of the teacher's mouth. That would be impossible and counterproductive. It means listening carefully for important points and then writing them down, even if the instructor doesn't. If you don't have time to finish writing down an important point, write down a few key words, then fill in the rest after class.

4) Be creative and develop your own style.

Notes don't have to be boring. Believe it or not, your notes can actually be a fun extension of who you are. You can develop your own unique style, and use your notes to express your creativity. A great way to accomplish this is to be creative when adding color and pictures to your notes. Develop your own color-coding scheme and icons to use in your notes. You can also develop your own shorthand, such as using "**?**" if you need to review something in more detail, or "**T**" if something is going to be on the test.

In addition, try experimenting with different types of notebooks and even how you format your notes. You don't necessarily have to start taking notes in the upper left-hand corner and work your way down. Try starting in the center and branching outwards. You can even rotate your entire notebook 90 degrees. And finally, experiment with different pens and pencils to find the ones you like. It's worth spending a little extra money to get quality writing instruments. You'll use them all the time, and it's a lot easier to be creative when you have the proper tools to work with.

5) Actively review your notes after class.

So far, we have learned one ninja note-taking technique to use before class starts and three techniques to use during class. This last one is used after class ends. The final note-taking technique is to actively review your notes after class. This means more than just rereading them once or twice. Active review requires the use of a pen or pencil. Your goal is to make sure your notes are as complete as possible. Here are a few things to consider when actively reviewing your notes:

- Make sure to fill in any gaps in your notes. Use the textbook, or borrow a classmate's notebook, to fill in any information you may have missed.

- Make sure that everything written in your notebook is legible and easy to understand. If something was not written clearly, there is a good chance it was not clearly understood.

- Make a note of anything you don't understand, so you can ask the teacher. Don't make the mistake of letting questions go unanswered. Since most classes are cumulative, misunderstandings tend to multiply if they are not cleared up in a timely fashion.

- Finally, use some of the time you spend actively reviewing to add color and images to your notes. This is also a great time to be creative as you develop your own personal style. Have fun and make your notes your ultimate study resource.

Ideally, we would spend 10 to 15 minutes reviewing our notes immediately after class, while the information is still fresh in our mind. If that's not possible because of scheduling, then review your notes as soon after class as possible.

These five simple techniques are easy to implement and will help you turn your notes into a powerful resource for academic success. Before I end this chapter, let me give you one final bonus strategy at no extra charge:

Turn off your cell phone during class.

You can't learn effectively or take quality notes if your attention is split between the instructor and your phone. Remember that there is no such thing as multitasking. Every time you check your email, text, or surf the web, your attention and focus shift. It will then take you time to shift your attention back to the class. This fragments the learning process - literally destroying recall. Study after study has shown that so-called multitasking hurts almost every aspect of academic performance. Put the phone away, or better yet, turn it off. Use your class time to focus on learning and taking quality notes using the techniques described above.

As a final note, you may be wondering why I called these "ninja note-taking techniques". The reason is because I really like the sound of it. ☺And also because these techniques are highly effective, as are ninjas.

> *"Ninjas are cool."*
> – Dr. Joe McCullough

Show You Know

1) Taking notes is important because it adds a _____ component to the learning process.

2) What is the one ninja note-taking technique you use before class starts?

3) What is the one ninja note-taking technique you use after class ends?

4) Ninjas are cool. True or False?

Answers:
1) Kinesthetic.
2) Preview the material before class.
3) Actively review your notes after class.
4) True!

Strategy #2: Read Faster (Five Simple Steps to Double Your Reading Speed)

"Reading is to the mind what exercise is to the body."
– Richard Steele

The average adult reads about 250 words per minute. This is much slower than most people are capable of reading. By using a few simple but effective techniques, you can easily increase your reading speed to 500 words per minute or faster. The five techniques presented below will allow you to double your reading speed (or more) with a minimal amount of effort.

1) Get into the right physical and mental space.

Have you ever tried to read a textbook or technical document while watching TV or at a loud coffee shop? It's not easy, is it? The constant distractions wreak havoc on your focus and can easily double or triple the amount of time it takes to read something. When you also consider the dramatic decrease in comprehension that occurs when reading with external distractions, it just doesn't make a lot of sense now, does it? If you are serious about reading quickly and comprehending what you read, make sure that you read in an environment free of external distractions.

This applies to internal distractions as well. How many times have you found your mind wandering in the middle of a paragraph? An easy way to counter internal distractions is to make sure that you are in a relaxed and focused state of mind. This corresponds to the alpha brain-wave state.

2) Eliminate subvocalization.

Subvocalization is when you say the words to yourself in your head as you read them. It is that inner voice that reads along with you and is one of the leading causes of slow reading. Think about it. If you silently say the words to yourself as you read, then your reading speed is limited by how fast you can talk. (Most people comfortably speak at about 150 words per minute; auctioneers generally speak 250-400 words per minute). If you are serious about speed reading, then reducing subvocalization is an absolute must! There are two techniques that I have found useful in helping to minimize subvocalization. The first is to just be aware that you are doing it, then make a conscious effort not to subvocalize. This is challenging and definitely takes practice - so be patient. The second technique is to force yourself to read much faster than you normally would, so your inner voice can't keep up. An awesome free application that you can use for this is AccelaReader, which uses Rapid Serial Visual Presentation to increase reading speed and minimize subvocalization.

3) Use a visual guide.

If you watch somebody's eyes while they read normally, you will notice that their eyes backtrack and make tiny bounces back and forth along the page. This "jerky" motion of the eyes, which is known as saccadic movements, greatly reduces reading speeds. The easiest way to eliminate this inefficient eye motion is to use your finger or a pen to guide your eyes as you read. This simple technique alone can double your reading speed.

To use your finger as a visual guide, place your finger directly below the word that you are reading. Move your finger smoothly across the page as you read and focus your eyes right above your finger. When you get to the end of a line, just move your finger to the beginning of the next line. You can control your reading speed by controlling the speed of your visual guide.

Using a visual guide also helps eliminate regression, which is the unnecessary rereading of words or sentences. In addition

to dramatically reducing reading speeds, regression can also reduce comprehension, because it interferes with the normal flow and meaning of the
words.

Simply using your finger as a visual guide can double your reading speed.

4) Read in chunks of 3-4 Words.

Almost everyone learned to read word-by-word, but this is not an efficient method of reading. Not only does reading one word at a time greatly reduce your reading speed, it also interferes with comprehension. This is because the meaning of a concept is conveyed by groups of words and not disconnected individual words. For example, when reading the words "up ……….. the ………….. creek …………. without ……… a …………… paddle" one word at a time, your brain must focus on the meaning of each word individually and then piece them all together. On the other hand, it is much easier for your brain to understand the meaning of "up the creek" "without a paddle" when the words are read in chunks.

The application AccelaReader mentioned above is a great resource to help train yourself to read in chunks of three or more words. It works by pasting the text you want to read into a textbox. You can then set your reading speed in words per minute and how many words you want displayed at once. The website www.spreeder.com has a similar application, as well as useful articles on speed reading.

5) Use your peripheral vision.

Even when you are looking straight ahead, your peripheral vision allows you to see off to either side. You can use this to your advantage to help you read faster. If you start at the first word of line of text and end on the last word, you are spending time reading the margins (where there is no text) with your peripheral vision. To counter this, you can use your visual guide to begin three words from the beginning of a line and finish three words from the end of a line.

Speed reading is a skill that can be mastered with a little practice. These five simple techniques will get you started. Good luck and happy reading!

Show You Know

1) The average adult has a reading speed of about how many words per minute?

   a) 200 words
   b) 250 words
   c) 300 words
   d) 350 words
   e) 400 words

2) I can read faster by using a few simple techniques. True or False?

3) What is subvocalization and why should it be avoided?

4) Simply using your _____ as a visual guide can double your reading speed.

Answers:

1) 250 words.
2) True.
3) Subvocalization is silently saying the words to yourself as you read. Subvocalization should be avoided because it limits your reading speed to how fast you can talk.
4) Finger.

Strategy #3: Set SMART Goals (Five Easy Strategies for Achieving SMART Goals)

"People with goals succeed because they know where they are going. It's as simple as that."

– Earl Nightingale

There are literally millions of articles, blogs, essays, mp3s, books, courses, and seminars on the topic of setting and achieving goals. I've taken many courses and seminars (some great and some not so great), and I'm well read on the subject. More importantly, I've personally experimented with many different techniques for almost two decades. I've enjoyed many great successes as well as many great learning opportunities. I'm here to tell you that setting and achieving goals boils down to a few simple concepts. I've decided to choose what I believe are the top five. These five simple strategies will help you set and achieve SMART goals, regardless how big they may seem.

Before we learn the five simple strategies, let's first make sure that our goals are SMART. SMART doesn't refer to the overall intelligence of our goal. SMART is an acronym that stands for Specific, Measurable, Attainable, Relevant, and Time-bound. These are important qualities of any well-formed goal. Let's take a quick look at each one.

Specific:

A specific goal is one that is clearly defined and unambiguous. The more specific your goal, the more likely you will be to accomplish it. This is because it's hard to wrap your brain around a vague goal, such as "I will be a better student". What exactly does it mean to be a better student? To be specific, a goal should be able to answer the five "W" questions:

- Who: *"Who is involved?"*
- What: *"What exactly do I want to accomplish?*
- When: *"When will it be finished by?"*
- Where: *"Where will I accomplish it?"*
- Why: *"Why is it important to me?"*

Measurable:

Ideally, a measurable goal has some kind of number or amount associated with it. This allows our brain to answer one of the most important questions in goal setting:

"How will I know when I have accomplished my goal?"

Some examples of measurable goals include: "I will go to the gym and lift weights for 45 minutes at least 3 days a week.", "I will complete 100% of my homework assignments in English on time.", and "I will finish the semester with a 3.50 GPA or better." Measurable goals answer questions such as *"How much?"*, *"How many?"*, and *"How often?"*. These are important questions to ask. A goal with a measurable outcome is much easier to track and manage.

"If you can't measure it, you can't manage it."

– Peter Drucker

Attainable:

When setting a goal, it is important to believe that the goal is within our reach. If we don't believe we can achieve a goal, we won't be motivated to put in the required time and effort. On the flip side of this, it is also important that the goal stretches us a bit. If the goal isn't a challenge, we run the risk of not being motivated to work toward something that is too easy. Ideally, we want the goal to be challenging, but not so hard that we get discouraged or believe it is out of reach.

Relevant:

Our goal must be personally relevant to us and our current life situation. We absolutely must know our WHY, and it must be personal. A relevant goal is one that is meaningful to us, one that **we ourselves** want to achieve. It is not a goal that someone else (a parent, a friend, a significant other …) wants for us. Personal relevance is important because it is virtually impossible to stay motivated and work hard to achieve someone else's goal.

In addition, our goal needs to be relevant to our current life situation. If you're a student with final exams coming up in two weeks, you probably won't be very motivated to accomplish a goal that doesn't have immediate relevance to your upcoming finals.

Time-bound:

Our goals need to have a time limit on them. This gives us a sense of urgency and helps us stay motivated. A goal without a time limit runs the risk of becoming a wish that we will get to someday. Goals can be short-term goals to be accomplished within a few weeks or long-term goals that may take several months or even years. Whatever the time scale, it is important to have an end date. Deadlines create a challenge, and we typically respond well to challenges.

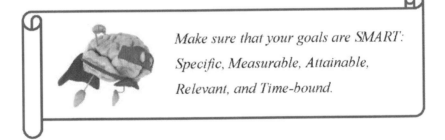

Make sure that your goals are SMART: Specific, Measurable, Attainable, Relevant, and Time-bound.

As you begin to create SMART goals, here are four guiding questions to ask yourself:

- *What do I want?*
- *Why do I want it?*
- *How will I know when I have it?*
- *Why don't I have it now?*

The answers to these questions will help you get clear on your goal and why you want to achieve it. Once you have a well-defined SMART goal, you can use the five strategies below to help you achieve it faster.

1) Believe you can do it.

As we learned in the first step of accelerated learning (Prepare your state), believing that you can and will be successful is an important ingredient for success. The same holds true for goal setting. If we set a goal that we don't believe we can achieve, we've failed before we've even started. In the immortal words of Yoda:

> Luke Skywalker: *"I don't believe it."*
> Yoda: *"That is why you fail."*

Believing we can do it doesn't mean that we won't have occasional doubts. However, deep down inside, we have to believe that we are capable of accomplishing our goal. Otherwise, there's a good chance that we'll quit once the going gets tough.

2) Have an initial plan.

Once we have a well-defined SMART goal that we believe we can achieve, one of the first things we want to do is to make an initial plan. Even if we don't know all of the steps to take, it's important to start with something. In the wise words of Winston Churchill, *"He who fails to plan is planning to fail."*

Here are four useful questions you can ask to help you develop an initial plan:

- *What are the first few steps that I need to take?*
- *What do I need to research and learn in order to accomplish my goal?*
- *Who do I know that can help me and offer support?*
- *What can I do within the next 24 hours that will move me forward?*

When planning for long-term goals, include smaller intermediate goals that can serve as milestones. Milestones are important because they give us a sense of progress and accomplishment as we work toward our long-term goal.

3) Post your goals where you can see them every day.

One of my biggest learnings after years of experimenting with goal setting is this:

Out of sight, out of mind.

Life can be hectic, and it's sometimes easy to lose sight of our goals. An effective way to prevent this is to remind ourselves of our goals on a daily basis. One of my most successful goal-setting strategies has been posting my goals where I can see them every single day. This can be accomplished using post-it notes, index cards, or even daily text reminders. Personally, I like to make 8.5 by 11 inch print outs of my goals, with lots of color and inspiring images. I then frame my goals and hang one next to my computer monitor at home, one in my office at school, and one over my toilet (sorry – too much information). I see my goals every day - which keeps them in my daily awareness. It also reminds me to take one small action toward each of my goals every day, which is one of the most effective goal-setting strategies there is.

4) Take action every day.

Please take a moment, and think about a long-term goal that you have. Think of a goal that may take you a year or more to accomplish. Do you have one? Good, then I have two quick questions for you. *Is this goal something that you are really committed to achieving? Are you willing to spend five minutes a day working toward achieving it?* If you answered yes to both of these questions, then your goal is as good as done (woo hoo!).

Imagine if you spent at least five minutes every day working toward your goal. Every day you took one small step forward. After one year, you'll have taken 365 actions toward accomplishing your goal. Think about how much progress you could make! Almost any goal can be achieved with consistent, daily effort. If you really want something, spending five minutes a day working toward getting it isn't much to ask.

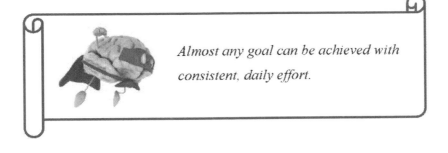

Almost any goal can be achieved with consistent, daily effort.

5) Get support from others.

One of the biggest mistakes I made when I first started setting goals was trying to do everything myself. I had this false belief that asking for help or support meant I wasn't able to do it myself. Because of this belief, I wasted a lot of time and energy struggling instead of using my available resources.

I now know that getting support and taking advantage of my available resources is one of the keys to achieving any goal. I have found two very effective ways of getting support:

First, find someone who has already accomplished what you want to achieve. Ask them what they did, how they did it, and if they have any advice for you. If someone can help you accomplish your goal in less time, you owe it to yourself to take advantage of their support. There is no need to reinvent the wheel. A second way of getting support is to have an accountability partner. This is someone you check in with on a regular basis and who will hold you accountable. The check-in can be a quick text, phone call, email, or even a Facebook post. The simple fact that you are updating someone else with your progress, can often provide the extra bit of motivation necessary to follow through, especially when you don't feel like it.

Once you have a SMART goal, you know your WHY, and you are willing to work for it, the last thing is to persevere and never give up! Sometimes the going gets tough ... that's alright. It's part of the process. If something that you tried didn't work, try something else. Now you know what doesn't work and you have a valuable piece of information. If your goal is something that you really want, don't let anything stop you. Success is there for those who are willing to work for it!

"Press on. Nothing in the world can take the place of persistence. Talent will not; nothing is more common than unsuccessful men with talent. Genius will not; unrewarded genius is almost a proverb. Education alone will not; the world is full of educated derelicts. Persistence alone is omnipotent."

- Calvin Coolidge

Show You Know

1) What does the acronym SMART stand for?

2) Believing you can do it is an important part of achieving your goals. True or False?

3) How often should you look at your goals?

   a) every day
   b) once a week
   c) once a month
   d) it doesn't really matter

4) When working toward a goal, it is best to do everything yourself without getting help and support from others. True or False?

Answers:

1) Specific, Measurable, Attainable, Relevant, and Time-bound.
2) True.
3) Every day. This keeps your goals in your awareness and reminds you to take daily action.
4) False. Use your available resources. Get help and support from family and friends.

Strategy #4: Manage Your Time (Ten Time-Management Tips for the Busy Student)

"Dost thou love Life? Then do not squander Time; for that's the stuff Life is made of."

– Benjamin Franklin

Everyone gets the same amount of time each and every day. We get 86,400 seconds; no more, no less. If we all get the same amount of time, why is it that some people accomplish so much more in a day than others? What do these productive and successful people have in common? This answer is quite simple. Successful people achieve more because they have learned how to use their time more efficiently. The key phrase in that last sentence is "learned how to". Time management is not a skill we are born with - it's a skill that must be learned and developed through practice.

Since this chapter is on time-management tips for the **busy student**, let's get right down to business. I've compiled what I believe are the top ten tips that any student in any class can use to manage their time more efficiently. These are techniques/strategies that you can apply right away. They don't require anything other than a willingness to accomplish more with your time.

1) Apply the 80/20 Principle.

The 80/20 Principle, also known as the Pareto Principle, is the cornerstone of effective time-management. It is also a valuable principle that can be applied to just about any area of life. The 80/20 Principle states the following:

80% of our results come from 20% of our efforts

In other words, all tasks are not created equally. A small fraction of the activities that we do on a daily basis produces the majority of our results. These are high-value tasks. The corollary to the 80/20 principle is that the other 80% of our efforts only produce 20% of our results. These are low-value tasks. Unfortunately, these are the activities that take up most of our time.

Determine which of your daily activities are low-value and which are high-value. Then commit to not working on low-value tasks while there are high-value tasks left unfinished. One of the keys to effective time management is knowing the value of every activity. Only then can we spend the majority of our time on the high-value tasks that produce most of our results.

All tasks are not created equally. 80% of our results come from 20% of our efforts.

2) Plan your day.

Starting our day with a clear plan of exactly what we want to accomplish is an easy way to get the most out of our 86,400 seconds. This is because long-term thinking improves short-term decision making. A clear plan guides our decisions as we navigate through the course of our day. Without a clear plan, it's easy to get swept up in the tide of life's many distractions.

A great time to plan your day is the night before. Spend five minutes before you go to bed thinking about your day tomorrow. Ask yourself the following two questions: *"What is the most important thing I need to accomplish tomorrow?"*, and *"What else do I need to do?"*. Rank your activities by importance … then make a plan for the day. Make sure to schedule your most important activities first. Write your plan down on paper, and then read it as soon as you wake up in the morning.

"Either you run the day or the day runs you."

– Jim Rohn

3) Practice proactive procrastination.

Every time we decide to do one thing, it means, by default, that we've decided not to do something else instead. If we really want to be more productive, then we have to make tough decisions about how we spend our time. We must decide to say no to low-value activities in favor of high-value ones. I like to think of this as practicing proactive procrastination. To do this, we continue to maintain an awareness that all tasks are not created equally. Then, we consciously decide which tasks to procrastinate on and which to take action on. We choose to procrastinate on our low-value activities, so we have more time to do the 20% that can make the real difference in our life.

"There is never enough time to do everything, but there is always enough time to do the most important thing."

– Brian Tracy

4) Schedule your power hour.

Earlier in the book, I mentioned that each of us tends to have a specific time of day when we're most focused/productive. A power hour is an uninterrupted 60-minute block of time, scheduled during this productive period, when we're really going to get down to business. I know that I've recommended working for 45 minutes at a time, but this is the exception. Our power hour is a focused 60 minutes, scheduled every single day, when we're going to tackle our most important tasks.

Hopefully, we've applied the 80/20 Principle and know which of our activities produce the majority of our results. These high-value tasks are the ones that we want to work on during our power hour. In essence, we are giving ourselves the best time of day to work on our most important activities. We start our power hour by attacking our highest-value task first. Work on this task and this alone! Don't try to multitask, and don't move on to another activity until this one is completed. If we finish our highest-value task, we then move on to the next most important one. We continue working on our high-value tasks until our power hour is up. Then we take a well-deserved break to relax and celebrate our efforts.

5) Prepare your state.

As we learned earlier, preparing our state is the very first step of accelerated learning. All of the techniques and strategies for getting into an optimal mental, emotional, and physical state for learning also apply to time management. Before we begin working on any task, an important first step is getting into an optimal state. Here are three quick steps you can use to prepare your state before starting any task:

1) Make sure that you have everything you need and that your workspace is well organized.

2) Do the alpha-state process to get into the alpha brain-wave state.

3) Know your outcome and your WHY. *What exactly are you going to accomplish, and why is it important?*

6) Take it one step at a time.

It can be easy to feel overwhelmed when we think about everything that must be done in order to complete a huge task. In fact, one of the major reasons that people procrastinate is because they feel overwhelmed by all that has to be done. When we take it one step at a time, we only concentrate on the immediate task at hand. We don't worry about what comes next. If there are several different projects that must be completed in order to accomplish a bigger task, we focus on the first project until it is finished. Only then do we move on to the next project on our list.

> *"Nothing is particularly hard if you divide it into small jobs."*
> – Henry Ford

Taking it one step at a time also means not trying to do two things at once - like trying to work and check email at the same time. This leads to our next time-management tip, limiting our use of electronics.

7) Limit your use of electronics.

I've said it before, and I'll say it again. Multitasking does not exist. Trying to work while, texting, checking email, or engaging in social media (Facebook, Twitter, Pinterest, etc.) severely reduces productivity. If we are serious about using our time more efficiently, then it is vital that we limit our distractions while working. An easy way to do this is to turn off all electronics that are not absolutely necessary to complete our work. This means putting away cell phones and only using the computer as needed. If we need to use the internet for research or as part of an assignment, we only keep one browser open, no Facebook and no email.

　　While we're on the subject of email, let me ask you a quick question. *How many times a day on average do you check email?* If the answer is more than two or three times, you have just identified a great opportunity to become more efficient. In most cases, there really is no need to check your email more than a couple of times a day. Try to develop the habit of only checking email twice a day, once in the morning and once in the evening. I know from personal experience that this can be challenging. However, the increase in your overall efficiency will be well worth the effort.

8) Recognize the law of diminishing returns.

The law of diminishing returns states that you eventually get less benefit from repeating the same task over and over. The return on the investment of your time is not worth the effort, and your time is better spent doing something different. Time management is all about getting the most bang (benefit) for your buck (time). Being busy doesn't necessarily mean you are being productive. Applying the law of diminishing returns means knowing when you should be doing something else. If what you're currently doing is no longer yielding your desired results, determine a better use of your time - then go and do it.

9) Use spare minutes wisely.

Here is a very revealing exercise that I highly encourage you to try. Take one full day, from the time you wake up until when you go to bed, and record how many "spare minutes" you have. A spare minute is one that you spend in between tasks or scheduled activities. For example, a spare minute would include any time that you spend waiting in line, commuting to school or work, driving in your car, using the bathroom, or walking between classes. This extra time can be used to your advantage. For students, a great way to use your spare minutes more efficiently is to always carry something with you to study. This can be class notes, index cards, study guides, anything you can read while you are waiting around (not while driving!).

Smart phones are a great resource to use when you have spare minutes. You can upload notes to such websites as Dropbox, Evernote or Google Drive. You can put all kinds of educational media (mp3s, videos, podcasts) on your phone to listen to. You can also record yourself reviewing class material and then listen to the recording during your commute. Be creative with your in-between time. Use these spare minutes wisely and you will have more minutes to enjoy other activities.

10) Ask yourself the all-important question.

The last tip is actually a question that I first learned from Brian Tracy. It is one of the most important questions that we can ask ourselves. We can ask it anytime, and the answer will always be helpful. Are you ready for it? OK, here is the all-important question:

What is the most valuable use of my time right now?

It's a simple question that is straight-forward and to the point. *What is the most valuable use of my time right now?* Once we know the answer, we'll know exactly how we should be spending our time. Now all we have to do is decide how we'll actually spend it.

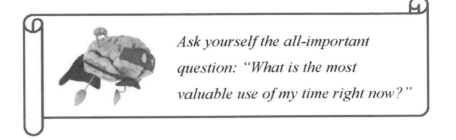

Ask yourself the all-important question: "What is the most valuable use of my time right now?"

Let's face it. We're all busy people with a lot on our plates. It would be great if we had unlimited time to do it all. But, as we all know, that's not going to happen. This means that in order to do more, we're going to have to be more efficient with the time we do have. The ten time-management tips presented above will help you do just that.

Managing your time more efficiently takes practice, but the results are so worth it. Every minute that we save by working more efficiently is a minute we can spend doing something else. Those extra minutes really add up once we get good at managing our time. Give these techniques a try for one week, and I know you'll agree.

Show You Know

1) The _____ Principle states that 80% of our results come from 20% of our efforts.

2) Preparing our state is an important part of time management. True or False?

3) Recognizing the law of _____ _____ means being aware of when our time is better spent doing something different.

4) What is the all-important question?

Answers:

1) 80/20 Principle or the Pareto Principle.
2) True.
3) Diminishing returns.
4) What is the most valuable use of my time right now?

Strategy #5: Eat Healthy (Ten Brain-Healthy Foods for Smarter Eating)

"To keep the body in good health is a duty, for otherwise we shall not be able to trim the lamp of wisdom, and keep our mind strong and clear."

~Buddha

Although on average the brain is only about 2% of the body's mass, it uses about 20% of the body's energy supply (i.e. calories). What we eat, therefore, has a tremendous impact on our brain and how well it functions. As you probably know, there are some foods that are much better for our bodies than others. The same is true for our brains. The following is a list (in no particular order) of ten foods that research has shown can have a positive impact on the health of our brain and on our cognitive abilities such as memory, focus, and problem solving.

1) Salmon

Most of the brain is made up of "good fats" know as fatty acids. Salmon, sardines, and other fish are high in brain-healthy Omega-3 fatty acids. These essential fatty acids are an important brain food that is vital for healthy brain function.

Recent studies have suggested that Omega-3's can enhance cognitive performance and improve short term memory.

2) Nuts and Seeds

Studies have shown that walnuts can enhance memory and improve brain functions. Other nuts such as almonds, pecans, and peanuts are also good sources of vitamin E, which may reduce cognitive decline associated with aging. Flax seeds and other seeds are a good source of brain-healthy Omega-3's.

3) Avocados

Avocados have monounsaturated fats, which help maintain the healthy blood flow necessary for a healthy brain. They are rich in oleic acid, which helps in the building of myelin, the insulation which surrounds the neurons in our brain.

4) Berries

Blueberries seem to be the rage now. I have even heard them referred to as "brain berries". I wouldn't go that far, but blueberries, raspberries, and other berries do contain powerful antioxidants that help protect the brain and that have been shown to improve memory and learning.

5) Spinach

Spinach is rich in antioxidants that help improve blood flow and protect the brain from damage caused by free radicals. Spinach is also packed with nutrients, such as folate, Vitamin-E, and Vitamin-K, that may slow age-related declines in cognitive ability and help prevent dementia. Research performed on rats has shown that rats fed a diet rich in spinach performed significantly better on memory/learning tests than rats fed a normal diet.

6) Whole Grains

Whole wheat, wheat germ, brown rice, and bran all contain folate, which helps increase blood flow to the brain. Whole-grain foods also contain B vitamins, which some studies suggest can improve memory.

7) Eggs

Eggs are full of essential fatty acids that are important for a healthy brain. The yoke itself is high in choline, a key nutrient necessary for normal brain development during pregnancy. Choline also plays an important role in memory function and has been shown to improve overall cognitive performance.

8) Freshly brewed tea

Freshly brewed black or green tea in the morning can be a great way to start your day. Both contain caffeine, which in modest amounts can enhance focus and memory, as well as mood. They also contain catechin, a potent antioxidant known to promote healthy brain function.

9) Chocolate

Yes, chocolate, dark chocolate especially, is good for the brain – in small amounts. The cacao beans found in dark chocolate have powerful antioxidants, which help protect your brain from harmful effects. Recent studies suggest that dark chocolate can improve blood flow to the brain and help you concentrate.

10) Red or purple grapes

Red and purple grapes (as well as red wine) contain resveratrol, which has been linked to improved blood circulation in the brain. Resveratrol is also known to mop up free radicals which can damage your cells (including brain cells). Since conventionally grown grapes are heavily sprayed, it is best to choose organic grapes whenever possible.

On a final note, maintaining proper hydration is important for both your body and your brain. Our brains rely on proper hydration in order to function optimally. Research has shown that dehydration can result in poor concentration, reduced cognitive abilities, and impaired memory. Remember to stay hydrated and include more brain-healthy foods in your diet.

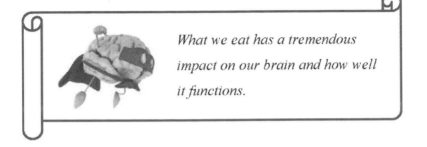

What we eat has a tremendous impact on our brain and how well it functions.

Show You Know

1) Although on average the brain is only about _____ % of the body's mass, it uses about _____ % of the body's energy supply (i.e. calories).

2) What we eat impacts our brain and how well it functions. True or False?

3) Which of the following food is not considered to be "brain-healthy"?

   a) Eggs.
   b) Chocolate.
   c) Avocados
   d) French fries.

4) Research has shown that _____ can result in poor concentration, reduced cognitive abilities, and impaired memory.

Answers:

1) 2% and 20%.
2) True.
3) French fries. As a general rule, if you can buy it at McDonalds or Burger King, it's not brain-healthy.
4) Dehydration.

Strategy #6: Be Happy (Ten Proven Ways to Increase Happiness)

"Success is not the key to happiness. Happiness is the key to success. If you love what you are doing, you will be successful."

– Albert Schweitzer

Many of us have been taught that if we work hard at school, land a good job and become successful, then we will be happy. In his ground-breaking book, *"The Happiness Advantage"*, Harvard psychologist Shawn Achor shows that this is actually backwards. It is not success that brings us happiness but the other way around. When we are happy, we are more likely to be successful. This holds true for all areas of life – at school, at work, and at home.

As we discussed earlier, our higher-order thinking skills, such as critical thinking and reasoning, become impaired whenever we feel negative emotions such as fear, anxiety, stress, or threat. Well, the opposite is true as well. When we feel positive emotions such as happiness, joy, and love, we have the greatest access to our higher intelligences. In essence, our brain functions most efficiently when we are happy.

This means that, as a student, you increase your chances of success by increasing your levels of happiness. Pretty cool, huh? You can do better at school by being a happier person.

So how does one become happier? There are numerous techniques that you can use. Listed below are ten proven techniques that will help you become a happier person and increase your chances of success in all areas of life.

1) Exercise Regularly.

Exercising on a regular basis, especially aerobic exercise, not only keeps our body and mind healthy, it also helps to improve our mood. Whenever we exercise, our body releases chemicals called endorphins that leave us feeling happier and more relaxed. In fact, exercise has such a beneficial effect on our mood, that it has been shown to be an effective treatment for depression. Regular exercise also promotes better sleep, which is another important factor in maintaining a positive mood.

2) Get a good night's sleep.

It is very difficult to function at our best when we are not well rested. As we learned earlier, sleep loss cripples thinking and long-term memory. You probably know from experience that sleep loss also negatively impacts our mood. Inadequate sleep can cause irritability, anxiety, stress, and mental exhaustion. Sleep loss has also been correlated with increased feelings of depression. When we don't get enough sleep, we're not only more prone to negative emotions, we're also less likely to reap the emotional benefits of a positive experience. Do yourself a favor – make sure that you get adequate rest. Your brain and your mood will thank you.

3) Spend time outdoors.

There is a strong link between positive moods and time spent outdoors. A series of studies published in the Journal of Environmental Psychology found that being outside in nature makes people feel happier and more alive. If you've ever spent time in a beautiful setting, such as a national park, you have probably experienced firsthand the uplifting effect that nature can have. The great thing is, nature doesn't have to be a stunning national park or scenic landscape. Simply being outdoors in the sunlight can dramatically decrease stress and increase happiness. There are other benefits as well. According to Dr. Susan Preston from South University, *"Research has shown that spending time in nature has been associated with decreased levels of mental illness, with the strongest links to reduced symptoms of depression and anxiety, in addition to increased self esteem."*

4) Spend time with friends and family.

In the famous study known as the Harvard Grant Study, researchers at Harvard University closely monitored the lives of 286 male undergraduates from the classes of 1938-1940 for 75 years. One of the goals of the longitudinal study was to determine the secrets to living a happy and fulfilled life. The results of this study show that one of the major predictors of happiness and fulfillment in life is the presence of close relationships with family and friends. The more quality time we can spend with those people who we love, the happier and more fulfilled we will be in our daily lives. In the words of George Valliant, who directed the study for more than thirty years, *"The seventy-five years and twenty million dollars expended on the Grant Study points to a straightforward five-word conclusion: 'Happiness is love. Full stop.' "*

5) Do something nice for someone else.

One of the easiest and most effective ways to quickly change your mood, if you are feeling sad or depressed, is to do something nice for someone else. When we help someone else, we often reap more benefit than the person we are helping. Numerous studies have shown that being kind to others makes us feel less stressed, happier and more connected to those around us. In one famous study, a group of students was asked to perform five random acts of kindness every week for a total of six weeks. Those students who performed the regular acts of kindness showed a 42% increase in happiness. Helping someone else can be very powerful – one study found that simply reflecting on nice things that we have done for others can elevate our mood.

On a related side note:

Every semester I give my students an extra credit assignment – perform a random act of kindness and then write a one-page essay on the experience. They can also choose to give out the card shown below to encourage the recipient to "pay it forward".

In their essays, all of my students report the experience as being a positive one that made them feel happy. Many of them also write that they plan on doing it again. I recently taped a bag of microwavable popcorn to a local Redbox with the card attached as a random act of kindness. It felt great at the time, and thinking back on it now makes me smile. Go out and try it yourself. You'll be glad that you did. It's fun and it will make you feel great! (Contact me at www.drjoemccullough.com and I will send you a few cards.)

6) Meditate.

It's been known for thousands of years that meditation can improve our well-being. Research has now proven this scientifically. Some of meditation's many benefits include improved focus, concentration, memory and attention span; decreased levels of stress and anxiety; and increased levels of happiness. The great thing is that you don't have to be a yogi to enjoy these benefits. Spending as little as 5 to 10 minutes a day in quiet meditation can have tremendous benefits on your health and happiness.

7) Practice gratitude.

It has often been said that the road to happiness starts with gratitude. This is because the simple act of recognizing and appreciating life, and the good things that people do for us, is an effective way of lifting our mood (as well as theirs). Expressing gratitude toward someone also deepens our relationship with them and reminds us that other people are there to support us. In studies conducted by Dr. Martin Seligman, the father of positive psychology, people who wrote letters of gratitude to someone who they had never properly thanked saw an immediate increase in happiness and decrease in depressive symptoms.

Here are two easy ways to practice gratitude that will make you feel great:

1) Express your gratitude toward at least one person every day for an entire week. Make it a different person each time, and make sure that you are specific when you express gratitude. Tell them exactly why you are grateful and what they mean to you. This can be done in person, over the phone, in a letter, or through email or text.

2) Start your day by recognizing and appreciating at least three things that you are grateful for in your life. You can say them silently to yourself, tell them to someone else, or write them down. Writing them in a gratitude journal is nice because you can always look back on all the things you are grateful for and immediately lift your mood.

8) Take note of your successes.

People often dwell on what is going wrong in their lives instead of what is going right. The problem with dwelling on the negative is that our brains look for what we focus on. If we look for what is going wrong in our lives, we will find it. The good news is that the flip side of this is also true. If we look for what is going right in our lives, we will find that instead.

An effective way to train your brain to look for what is going right in your life is to take note of your successes on a regular basis. I recommend that you recognize and acknowledge your successes daily. For the best results, acknowledge at least three successes and put them in writing. My friend and I have been emailing our successes to each other every night for the last five years. (We also email at least one thing that we are grateful for.) Taking note of my successes has been such an awesome experience for me that I now give all my classes an extra credit assignment of keeping a success journal. Every day for thirty days, they must reflect back on their day and write down at least three successes. I have had many students enjoy this so much that they are still doing it today.

9) Forgive.

Most of us know from experience that it's very hard to be happy when we're upset or angry with someone. Holding onto a grudge, more often than not, causes us more pain than the other person. It takes us out of the now as we replay the past injustices inflicted upon us. It also dramatically decreases our overall happiness.

Forgiving someone, when we feel wronged, is often easier said than done. However, keep in mind that forgiveness is a choice, one that will lower our stress levels and move us closer to happiness. And the happier we are, the more successful we'll be in all areas of life. Seems like a pretty good choice now, doesn't it?

"Forgive all who have offended you, not for them, but for yourself."

- Harriet Nelson

10) Stay present (live in the moment).

"Stop and smell the roses."

"Live for the moment."

"Enjoy the here and now."

"Seize the day."

These are all different ways of saying the same thing: stay present and live in the now. Spiritual teachers have been teaching their students to stay present for thousands of years. And, for thousands of years, students have struggled to consistently implement this teaching. I know from personal experience that staying present can be challenging. Many of us have a tendency to dwell in the past or worry about the future, both of which take us away from the here and now. Sometimes we do this because we fear that happiness is somewhere else. Sometimes we do it out of habit. Whatever the reason, when we miss out on the present moment, we miss out on a lot. Life happens in the now, not in the past or future. Stay present, embrace the now, and enjoy all that life has to offer you in this present moment.

"The secret of health for both mind and body is not to mourn for the past, not to worry about the future, or not to anticipate troubles, but to live in the present moment wisely and earnestly."

— Buddha

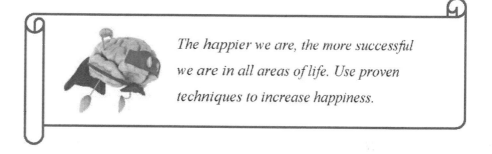

The happier we are, the more successful we are in all areas of life. Use proven techniques to increase happiness.

Show You Know

1) When we are _____, we are more likely to be successful.

2) The result of the 75 year Harvard Grant Study showed that one of the major predictors of happiness was close relationships with family and friends. True or False?

3) What is at least one technique from this chapter that you are willing to try in order to become a happier person?

4) What is another technique you are willing to try?

Answers:

1) Happy.
2) True. According to George Valliant, "*Happiness is love. Full stop.*"
3) Try it tomorrow.
4) Use both techniques the next day. If you feeling adventurous, add a third technique the next day, and then another technique every day for a week.

Part 3:
Closing Thoughts and
Bonus Resources

Closing Thoughts

"There is no end to education. It is not that you read a book, pass an examination, and finish with education. The whole of life, from the moment you are born to the moment you die, is a process of learning."
                                                            – Jiddu Krishnamurti

So here we are near the end; our adventure is just about over. I truly appreciate you taking the time to read this book. I hope you enjoyed reading it as much as I enjoyed writing it (at least most of the time).

Before we finish our journey together, let me leave you with two final thoughts. First, please take a moment to think about how many hours you've spent learning various subjects throughout your academic career. If you're a high school or college student, the number is in the thousands. Now, take a moment to consider how much time you've spent learning how you learn best. For many students, they can count on one hand the number of hours they've spent learning how they learn best. This is unfortunate because knowing how to learn quickly and efficiently is one of the most valuable skills you can have.

Do yourself a favor and use the accelerated learning techniques presented in this book. They **will** help you learn more in less time. Every hour of studying you save is an extra hour you can spend doing something else. Remember, it's not the quantity of time you spend studying, but the quality of time. How you study is **way** more important than how much you study.

The final thought that I want to leave you with is the following:

You **can** become great at anything you want!

The strategies and techniques presented in this book aren't just for academic subjects. They apply to any skill. It doesn't matter if you are learning how to play guitar, skydive, or knit a sweater. These techniques will help you learn faster and with less effort. You might even have more fun along the way. Give them a try. You have nothing to lose and everything to gain.

You are a genius and these techniques will help you unlock it. I'm not kidding. You just learned some life-changing strategies. Go out and start using them today!

"It's a funny thing about life; if you refuse to accept anything but the very best, you very often get it."
– Somerset Maugham

Bonus Resource 1:
Top 20 Tips for Student Success

For the faithful readers who have made it this far, I want to give you some bonus resources. They are my way of saying thanks again for buying this book and taking the time to read it.

The first bonus is a list of my top 20 tips for student success. These tips are the result of my 16+ years of teaching high school and college. They are the strategies that I've consistently observed the most successful students using to succeed in all their classes. These tips are not specific to any particular subject. They can be used by any student, in any class, to become more successful.

1) Prepare an optimal learning space.
As we learned previously, where we work can have a significant impact on how well we learn. Keep in mind, a disorganized workspace often leads to disorganized thinking and work habits. Take an objective look at your work space and ask yourself, *"What kind of student would work in this environment?"*

2) Plan your day on paper.
Take a few minutes each night to plan the next day on paper. Write down when, and where, you are going to study and work on class assignments. Make sure to schedule your most

important tasks during your power hour. As you plan your day, remember to include time to relax and exercise, as well.

3) Know how you will use your "spare minutes".

Recall that "spare minutes" are time you spend commuting, in line, or in between scheduled activities. These spare minutes are gifts of time you can use to become more productive. When planning your day, make sure you know exactly how you will use your spare minutes.

4) Get to know your teachers.

Teachers are people too; get to know them. Introduce yourself the first week of school, either after class or during office hours. You will stand out as a serious student who wants to succeed. In addition, the personal connection with your instructor may increase your motivation in their class.

5) Always know your grade in every class.

As a student, you always want to know where you stand in every class. You never want to be surprised with your grade at the end of the quarter/semester. Read the class syllabus and know exactly how your teacher grades. Enter every grade that you receive into a spreadsheet and periodically check in with your instructor.

6) Read the textbook before class.

Reading the textbook before class is one the most important student success strategies there is. Although all students know they should, very few of them actually do. Reading the textbook before class gives your brain the big picture, introduces you to the concepts you'll be learning, and allows you to ask intelligent questions during class.

7) Go to every class.

This is your education. You are paying for it! Don't miss class, even if the instructor is boring. If you absolutely must miss class, make sure to contact the teacher and arrange to get the notes from a classmate.

8) Sit front and center during class.

Studies show that there is a direct correlation between a student's grades and where they sit in the classroom. Students who sit front and center consistently score higher than those who sit at or near the back. The simple act of sitting closer to the front (and center) of the classroom can improve your grades.

9) Take great notes.

Great students take great notes. It really is as simple as that. If you want to improve your grades in any class, an easy first step is to improve the quality of your class notes. Turn off your cell phone during class and focus on using your ninja note-taking techniques.

10) Know your preferred learning style(s) and intelligence(s).
Knowing how you learn best can save you hundreds of hours of studying over the course of your academic career. Spend the time required to really figure out how you learn best. Develop your own "learning toolkit" that you can use to master any subject.

11) Model other successful students.
As Tony Robbins likes to say, *"Success leaves clues."* There's no need to reinvent the wheel. Find someone who has done well in the classes you are taking, and ask them how they did it.

12) Don't wait until the last minute.
One of the habits almost all unsuccessful students have in common is that they wait until the last minute to do everything. They start the homework the night before it is due, they put off writing papers until the very last minute, and they cram for every quiz or exam. If you want to enjoy more academic success, it is imperative that you break this bad habit. Complete all assignments at least one day before they are due, and prepare for exams at least a few days in advance.

13) Find a study partner or group.
One of the most effective ways to learn something is to teach it to someone else. This is one of the reasons why studying with a group or partner is so effective. Just make sure to stay focused on the task at hand. Don't spend so much time socializing that you don't accomplish what you need to get done.

14) Maintain healthy habits.

As a student, it is often easy to get so focused on your studies that you forget about the other areas of life. While this may work in the short term, in the long term, it will eventually lead to burn out. Life is all about balance. Make sure you eat healthy, exercise, and get a good night's sleep. Your brain and your body will thank you.

15) Believe in yourself.

Believing in yourself and your abilities is one of the most important beliefs you can have. This is especially true as a student. If you don't believe that you can succeed, it will be easy to get discouraged when things get tough.

16) Manage your state.

Your mental, emotional, and physical states are all connected. If you change one, you change them all. One of the most valuable skills you can have is the ability to adjust your state as needed. For example, the alpha-state process is a great way to get into the optimal state before studying or taking a test.

17) Consider the consequences of your decisions.

Where you are today is the direct result of the decisions you've made up until now. Where you'll be five years from now will be based upon the decisions you make between now and then. Consider the consequences of your decisions; your future depends upon it!

18) Use your available resources.

Most schools have a tremendous number of resources available to help you succeed. These include study centers, tutors, academic advisers, counselors, instructors, and fellow students. Take responsibility for your own education and use your available resources!

19) Celebrate all successes.

It's not uncommon for students to feel like they're trapped on a never-ending treadmill of school work. A soon as one assignment is finished, there are still three others that need attention. One of the reasons students feel overwhelmed and stressed during the school year is that they don't take the time to reward their efforts. Anytime you finish an assignment, big or small, take time to celebrate your success.

20) Ask yourself the all-important question.

As a reminder, the all-important question is: *"What is the most valuable use of my time right now?"* The answer to this simple question will help you determine the most beneficial use of your time.

And as bonus bonus, I'll leave you with one final student success tip.

Use the accelerated learning techniques presented in this book!

You now know how to learn more in less time. Use that knowledge! To quote Forrest Gump,

"And that's all I have say about that."

Bonus Resource 2:
Killer Websites for Student Success

The websites listed below will support you on your journey toward academic mastery. Use them in conjunction with the information presented in this book, and you'll have all the resources necessary to succeed in any class.

Websites to help you succeed in school:

www.DrJoeMcCullough.com
I have to give my web site a shout out here. I have great resources on accelerated learning and life skills, including my monthly blog. I also plan on adding free video content in the near future. Sign up for my quarterly newsletter to stay informed of future updates and new learning resources.

www.MindTools.com
Mind Tools offers a wide variety of useful resources for both academic and life success. Many of them are available for free. There are articles covering goal setting, learning styles, memory techniques, decision making, and other important topics.

www.hackcollege.com

As the Hack College website states: "work smarter, not harder". This site contains all kinds of useful tips to help you succeed in college.

www.calnewport.com/blog

This is Cal Newport's Study Hacks Blog. Cal is the author of *"How to Become a Straight-A Student"*, as well as several other books. His site has some great articles on how to study more effectively.

www.how-to-study.com

This site was created by two former university professors. It contains helpful articles on study skills, but the real gem is hundreds of great study tips submitted by users just like you.

www.ou.edu/studentsuccess.html

This is the University of Oklahoma's student success website. It has good information on note taking, reading comprehension, time management, and study spaces.

Websites with online classes and tutorials:

www.khanacademy.org

Sal Kahn created Khan Academy in order to provide free, world-class education to anyone anywhere. Students can access an extensive library of lessons, videos, and assessments covering hundreds of different subjects.

www.ocw.mit.edu

MIT OpenCourseWare is an amazing resource based upon a simple concept – publish all MIT course information online and make it freely available to everyone. If you've ever wanted to take a class at MIT, here is your chance to do it from the comfort of your own home.

www.coursera.org

Coursera offers hundreds of free, online courses covering a wide-array of subjects. From nanotechnology to Buddhism and modern psychology, you can take classes from some of the best college instructors in the world.

www.YouTube.com

I'm sure you know about YouTube for the endless number of distracting videos featuring cute kittens and babies. I hope you also know about the tremendous number of excellent educational videos, as well. Just make sure you find a reliable source you can trust.

www.ted.com

As the website states, 1700+ talks to stir your curiosity. You can't go wrong with these short talks by some of the most intelligent and talented people on the planet. Be sure to also check out TED-Ed (ed.ted.com). This relatively new site allows users to create and share lessons around any TED talk or YouTube video.

Website to help you organize and study:

www.google.com
I'm sure you know about Google for web searches and for Gmail. Do you also know about Google Calendar, Google Drive, Google Scholar, Google Alerts, and Google Hangouts? Google provides an abundance of free, customizable tools to help you stay organized across all your mobile devices.

www.evernote.com
Evernote is a great program you can use to take well-organized, ninja-style notes. Evernote allows you to create text, photo and audio notes, insert web pages into your notes, and synchronize them across your various devices.

www.quizlet.com
Quizlet offers simple tools to help you study. You can create free, flash-card-based quizzes you can access online or with your smart phone.

www.hippocampus.org
This site offers free educational resources for high school and college students, which are nicely organized by subject. In addition, it has a very cool name. ☺

Websites with information on valuable life skills:

www.Success.com
I love Success Magazine and have been a subscriber for many years. Success.com is the official website of the magazine. It has great resources and valuable information on all areas of success.

www.topachievement.com
This is one of the top self-improvement sites on the internet. It has practical articles on goal setting, self-improvement, relationships, and motivation.

www.selfgrowth.com
This popular self-improvement site has over 300,000 articles on personal development. From success skills to mental health, this comprehensive site has something for everyone.

www.fourhourworkweek.com
This site is the official blog of Timothy Ferris. He is the author of *The Four Hour Workweek, The Four Hour Body,* and *The Four Hour Chef.* He has some very interesting things to say about rapidly learning and mastering any new skill.

Bonus Resource 3:
Calling All Callouts

The callouts interspersed throughout this book were included to reinforce key points that I felt deserved special attention. Since these callouts emphasized the most important point(s) from each chapter, I thought it would be a useful resource to have them all together in one place. For that reason, I've listed all callouts below in order of appearance. You can spend a few minutes reading through them at any time to remind yourself of the most important aspects of accelerated learning.

When we feel fear, anxiety, stress, or threat, we have very little access to our higher-order thinking skills.

Positive emotions such as fun, joy, and excitement are important for both learning and memory.

We create stronger and more permanent memories when we store the information using all of our senses.

The alpha brain-wave state is the optimal brain-wave state to be in for learning.

The 5 steps of accelerated learning can be remembered with the acronym **PACER**.

We can double our learning by spending just 5 to 10 minutes preparing our state.

The alpha brain-wave state is the optimal brain-wave state to be in for learning. Yes, I said it again!

The bigger your WHY, the easier your HOW!

Where you study can have a significant effect on how well you learn.

Starting with the big picture makes the learning process more efficient and increases recall.

Incorporating multiple learning modalities (VAK) into every study session will deepen your learning and increase recall.

Everyone learns differently. You can develop you own "learning toolkit" by experimenting with different learning techniques and strategies.

Deliberately connecting new information to old information creates associations and enhances memory.

The more senses you use while learning, the stronger the memory will be stored.

We tend to remember information that stands out from the rest. Adding color and images to your notes can make them more memorable.

Multitasking does not exist. Listening to music with lyrics while studying splits our attention and decreases recall.

Sleep loss cripples thinking and long-term memory. A good night's sleep is crucial to your success.

When you examine your knowledge, make sure to have fun and incorporate accelerated learning techniques.

Practices makes permanent. Be careful what you practice because you might get good at it!

Your personal learning style is as unique as your fingerprint. Learning how you learn best requires reflection and revision.

Celebrate immediately after an accomplishment. Don't wait and don't start a new task without rewarding your efforts.

Your notes are perhaps your greatest single tool for success in any class. Everyone should take notes during class.

Simply using your finger as a visual guide can double your reading speed.

Make sure that your goals are SMART: Specific, Measurable, Attainable, Relevant, and Time-bound.

Almost any goal can be achieved with consistent, daily effort.

All tasks are not created equally. 80% of our results come from 20% of our efforts.

Ask yourself the all-important question: "What is the most valuable use of my time right now?"

What we eat has a tremendous impact on our brain and how well it functions.

The happier we are, the more successful we are in all areas of life. Use proven techniques to increase happiness.

Bonus Resource 4:
Quoting All Quotes

I love sharing good quotes with my students. To me, quotes are little nuggets of knowledge – words of wisdom wrapped up in a sentence or two. That's one reason I included so many throughout this book. I also love reading books that have quotes interspersed throughout the text. However, I've always wished that books would list all quotes in one place for easy reference. Since this is my book, I've decided to do just that. Listed below is every quote I used in order of appearance. There are some really great ones. Enjoy!

"Success happens not by chance, but because you were given a chance and took advantage of it." – Kevin Geary

"If you wanted to create an educational environment that was directly opposed to what the brain was good at doing, you would probably design something like a classroom". – Dr. John Medina

"The brain is a monstrous, beautiful mess. Its billions of nerve cells - called neurons - lie in a tangled web that displays cognitive powers far exceeding any of the silicon machines we have built to mimic it." – William F. Allman

"The number of possible interconnections between these cells (neurons) is greater than the number of atoms in the universe". – Robert Ornstein and Richard Thompson

"Live as if you were to die tomorrow. Learn as if you were to live forever." – Mahatma Gandhi

"Before anything else, preparation is the key to success." – Alexander Graham Bell

"It is our attitude at the beginning of a difficult task which, more than anything else, will affect its successful outcome." – William James

"Whether you think you can, or whether you think you can't, either way, you are usually right." – Henry Ford

"Believe in yourself, and the rest will fall into place. Have faith in your own abilities, work hard, and there is nothing you cannot accomplish." – Brad Henry

"I don't care how much power, brilliance or energy you have, if you don't harness it and focus it on a specific target, and hold it there you're never going to accomplish as much as your ability warrants." – Zig Ziglar

"How you study is WAY more important than how much you study." – Dr. Joe McCullough

"You don't understand anything until you learn it more than one way." – Marvin Minsky

"Everyone is a genius. But if you judge a fish on its ability to climb a tree, it will live its whole life believing that it is stupid."
– Albert Einstein

"No matter what the level of your ability, you have more potential than you can ever develop in a lifetime." – James T. McCay

"You never realize what a good memory you have until you try to forget something." – Franklin P. Jones

"Tell me and I forget, teach me and I may remember, involve me and I learn." – Benjamin Franklin

"The bottom line is that sleep loss means mind loss. Sleep loss cripples thinking, in just about every way you can measure thinking. Sleep loss hurts attention, executive function, working memory, mood, quantitative skills, logical reasoning ability, and general math knowledge." – Dr. John Medina

"Memory is the treasury and guardian of all things." – Cicero

"The unexamined life is not worth living." – Socrates

"People rarely succeed unless they have fun in what they are doing."
– Dale Carnegie

"I've missed more than 9000 shots in my career. I've lost almost 300 games. 26 times, I've been trusted to take the game winning shot and

missed. I've failed over and over and over again in my life. And that is why I succeed." – Michael Jordan

"Anyone who has never made a mistake has never tried anything new." –Albert Einstein

"An expert is a person who has made all the mistakes that can be made in a very narrow field." – Niels Bohr

"Celebrate what you want to see more of." – Tom Peters

"Without continual growth and progress, such words as improvement, achievement, and success have no meaning." – Benjamin Franklin

"The more you praise and celebrate your life, the more there is in life to celebrate." – Oprah Winfrey

"Experience has taught me that there is one chief reason why some people succeed and others fail. The difference is not one of knowing, but of doing. The successful man is not so superior in ability as in action. So far as success can be reduced to a formula, it consists of this: doing what you know you should do." – Roger Babson

"Successful people aren't born that way. They become successful by establishing the habit of doing things that unsuccessful people don't like to do. The successful people don't always like these things themselves; they just get on and do them." – Steve Ibbotson

"But wait, there's more!" – Ron Popeil

"Attending lectures without taking notes is like keeping your mouth open and hoping for a roast duck to fly in." – R. Hummel

"Ninjas are cool." – Dr. Joe McCullough

"Reading is to the mind what exercise is to the body."
– Richard Steele

"People with goals succeed because they know where they are going. It's as simple as that." – Earl Nightingale

"If you can't measure it, you can't manage it." – Peter Drucker

Luke Skywalker: *"I don't believe it."*
Yoda: *"That is why you fail."*

"He who fails to plan is planning to fail." – Winston Churchill

"Press on. Nothing in the world can take the place of persistence. Talent will not; nothing is more common than unsuccessful men with talent. Genius will not; unrewarded genius is almost a proverb. Education alone will not; the world is full of educated derelicts. Persistence alone is omnipotent." – Calvin Coolidge

"Dost thou love Life? Then do not squander Time; for that's the stuff Life is made of." – Benjamin Franklin

"Either you run the day or the day runs you." – Jim Rohn

"There is never enough time to do everything, but there is always enough time to do the most important thing." – Brian Tracy

"Nothing is particularly hard if you divide it into small jobs." – Henry Ford

"To keep the body in good health is a duty, for otherwise we shall not be able to trim the lamp of wisdom, and keep our mind strong and clear." – Buddha

"Success is not the key to happiness. Happiness is the key to success. If you love what you are doing, you will be successful." – Albert Schweitzer

"Research has shown that spending time in nature has been associated with decreased levels of mental illness, with the strongest links to reduced symptoms of depression and anxiety, in addition to increased self esteem." – Dr. Susan Preston

"The seventy-five years and twenty million dollars expended on the Grant Study points to a straightforward five-word conclusion: 'Happiness is love. Full stop.'" – George Valliant

"Forgive all who have offended you, not for them, but for yourself." – Harriet Nelson

"The secret of health for both mind and body is not to mourn for the past, not to worry about the future, or not to anticipate troubles, but to live in the present moment wisely and earnestly." – Buddha

"There is no end to education. It is not that you read a book, pass an examination, and finish with education. The whole of life, from the moment you are born to the moment you die, is a process of learning." – Jiddu Krishnamurti

"It's a funny thing about life; if you refuse to accept anything but the very best, you very often get it." – Somerset Maugham

"Success leaves clues." – Tony Robbins

"And that's all I have say about that." – Forrest Gump

Bibliography

Achor, Shawn. *The Happiness Advantage: The Seven Principles of Positive Psychology that Fuel Success and Performance at Work*. New York: Crown Publishing, 2010 (ISBN: 978-0307591548)

Ambrose, Susan et al. *How Learning Works: 7 Research-Based Principles for Smart Teaching*. San Francisco: Wiley and Sons, 2010 (ISBN: 978-0470484104)

Coyle, Daniel. *The Talent Code: Greatness Isn't Born. It's Grown. Here's How*. New York: Bantam Dell, 2009 (ISBN: 978-0553806847)

Churches, Richard and Terry, Roger. *NLP for Teachers: How to be a Highly Effective Teacher*. Bethel, CT: Crown House Publishing, 2007 (ISBN: 978-1845900632)

DePorter, Bobbi. *Quantum Learning: Unleashing the Genius in You*. New York, New York: Dell Publishing, 1992. (ISBN: 978-0440504276)

Doidge, Norman. *The Brain that Changes Itself: Stories of Personal Triumph from the Frontiers of Brain Science*. London: Penguin Books, 2007 (ISBN: 978-0143113102)

Dweck, Carol. *Mindset: The New Psychology of Success*. New York: Ballantine Books, 2006. (ISBN: 978-0345472328)

EduNova, *The Most Complete Student Success System*. (http://www.edu-nova.com) Orange Duck Publishers, 2012. (ISBN: 978-1467512329)

Gardner, Howard. *Frames of Mind: The Theory of Multiple Intelligences*. New York, New York: Basic Books, 1993. (ISBN: 978-0465024339)

Gardner, Howard. *Multiple Intelligences, New Horizons.* New York, New York: Basic Books, 2006. (ISBN: 978-0465047680)

Lorayne, Harry and Jerry Lucas, *The Memory Book: The Classic Guide to Improving Your Memory at Work, at School, and at Play*. New York: Ballantine Books, 1986 (ISBN: 978-0345337580)

Medina, John. *Brain Rules: 12 Principles for Surviving and Thriving at Work, Home, and School.* Seattle: Pear Press, 2009 (ISBN: 978-0979777745)

Medina, John. *Brain Rules for Baby: How to Raise a Smart and Happy Baby from Zero to Five*. Seattle: Pear Press, 2010 (ISBN: 978-0983263302)

Meier, Dave. *The Accelerated Learning Handbook: A Creative Guide to Designing and Delivering Faster, More Effective Training Programs*. New York: McGraw-Hill, 2000 (ISBN: 978-0071355476)

Newport, Cal. *How to Become a Straight-A Student: The Unconventional Strategies Real College Students Use to Score High While Studying Less*. New York: Broadway Books, 2007 (ISBN: 978-0767922715)

Pauk, Walter and Ross Owens. *How to Study in College*. Wadsworth: Cengage Learning, 2010 (ISBN: 978-1439084465)

Paul, Kevin. *Study Smarter, Not Harder*. North Vancouver, BC: Self-Council Press, 2009. (ISBN: 978-1551808499)

Rose, Colin and Malcolm Nichol. *Accelerated Learning for the 21st Century*. New York, New York: Dell Publishing, 1997. (ISBN: 978-0440507796)

Sousa, David. *How the Brain Learns*. Thousand Oaks, CA: Corwin Press, 2011. (ISBN: 978-1412997973)

Tracy, Brian. *Eat That Frog: 21 Great Ways to Stop Procrastinating and Get More Done in Less Time*. San Francisco: Berrett-Koehler Publishers, 2007 (ISBN: 978-1576754221)

Tracy, Brian. *Goals! How to Get Everything You Want - Faster Than You Ever Thought Possible*. San Francisco: Berrett-Koehler Publishers, 2010 (ISBN #: 978-1605094113)

Willis, Judy. *Research-Based Strategies to Ignite Student Learning*. Alexandria: ASCD, 2006 (ISBN: 978-1416603702)

Wyman, Pat. *Amazing Grades: 101 Best Ways to Improve Your Grades Faster*. Las Vegas: The Center for New Discoveries in Learning, 2012 (ISBN: 978-1890047009)

About the Author

Dr. Joe McCullough began teaching physics at Cabrillo College near Santa Cruz, CA nearly thirteen years ago. He soon found himself concerned by the number of students experiencing test-taking anxiety and other school-related phobias. *Could anything be done to help them?* Joe began studying the brain and Neuro-Linguistic Programming – eventually becoming a certified Destination Coach – determined to make a difference. Little did he know, this desire to resolve school-related anxieties was only the beginning of a decade-long fascination with the brain and how people learn!

Today, Joe is Cabrillo College's Physics Program Chair. He has undergone hundreds of hours of training in neuroscience, accelerated learning techniques, and brain-based teaching methods. He's also a certified trainer and former facilitator for SuperCamp and Quantum Learning Network. In his spare time, Joe is a dedicated husband, father, avid outdoorsman, and amateur magician.

This book was born from Joe's passion for teaching and commitment to helping students everywhere learn more in less time. For more information, please visit:

www.drjoemccullough.com.

Made in the USA
Charleston, SC
21 March 2015